Prophecy, behaviour and change

Library of Social Work

General Editor:
Noel Timms
Professor of Social Work Studies
University of Newcastle upon Tyne

Prophecy, behaviour and change

An examination of self-fulfilling prophecies in helping relationships

Gerald G. Smale
Centre for Continuing Education
University of Sussex

Routledge & Kegan Paul
London, Henley and Boston

First published in 1977
by Routledge & Kegan Paul Ltd
39 Store Street,
London WC1E 7DD,
Broadway House,
Newtown Road,
Henley-on-Thames,
Oxon RG9 1EN and
9 Park Street,
Boston, Mass. 02108, USA
Set in 10 on 11 pt English
and printed in Great Britain by
The Lavenham Press Limited
Lavenham, Suffolk

ISBN 0 7100 8470 6

To my Mother and Father

Contents

Preface   ix

1 Introduction   1
The need for a new theoretical framework   2
Core themes in helping relationships   5
Variables affecting change   7
Toward an eclectic framework   9
Preview of discussion   12

2 The self-fulfilling prophecy   16
Expectations, prognostic expectations and self-
fulfilling prophecies   16
The three stages of the self-fulfilling prophecy   19
Characteristics of self-fulfilling prophecies   20
Self-fulfilling prophecies and labelling theory   21

3 Bias, hypnosis and placebos   25
Experimenter and teacher bias   25
Hypnosis   29
Placebos   32
Conclusions   37

4 Prophecy in helping relationships   40
Is psychotherapy a placebo?   40
The role of hope   42
Expectations and behaviour in helping
relationships   45
Conclusions   51

Contents

5 **Behaviour and change**   52
   The communication of expectations   52
   Reinforcement and prophecy fulfilment   54
   Modelling and prophecy fulfilment   57

6 **Client-centred therapy: an example**   60
   The prophecy   60
   The behaviour   63
   The outcome   66

7 **How to maximise the prophet's potency**   68
   Status, personality and specific behaviour   68
   The matching of helper and client expectations   72
   The client and conflicting expectations   73
   The level of expectations   74
   Setting optimum conditions   75

8 **For better or for worse**   77
   The debate reviewed   77
   Helpful and harmful prophets   81
   Outcome and choice   83

9 **Prophecy and practice**   86

   Bibliography   97

Preface

The seeds of this book were sown in my experience as a Probation Officer. I became increasingly concerned by the differences in outcome of colleagues' cases. One colleague believed in the psychological roots of all 'disorders' and often referred cases to psychiatrists. When he left the office it became apparent that his caseload did contain what seemed to be a significantly high proportion of 'mentally disturbed' clients!

Two other officers were young and had similar training and backgrounds. Yet their views differed dramatically on how to help drug addicts—and so did their results! One was optimistic and believed he could help these clients in the community. The other felt that the help he could offer and the resources that he could mobilise were totally inadequate and that these cases were doomed to fail. Over the course of a couple of years it became more and more apparent that their respective clients were showing quite different results. The optimist had mainly kept his clients in the community— the pessimist's had nearly all gone into institutions of one sort or another, usually as a result of a dramatic deterioration in their condition.

Could it be that the variety of outcome was a direct result of the differences between the professional helpers? Were these clients in some way living up to the expectations of their supervising officers?

The work of Rosenthal reawakened these ideas and suggested the possibility of presenting the concept of the self-fulfilling prophecy with more than anecdotal evidence.

Preface

As will become apparent during the discussion, I have also relied on the work of other writers notably Jerome Frank and A. P. Goldstein for their views and evidence on hope and expectations in psychotherapy, T. X. Barber's work on hypnosis, and A. K. Shapiro's extensive review of placebo literature. However, it is Carl Rogers' work and that of Truax and Carkhuff which have probably had the greatest overall impact upon my thinking in these areas.

I have attempted to present evidence which shows that self-fulfilling prophecies may be of crucial significance both for better and for worse in helping relationships. The primary aim is to highlight the expectations of the therapist as an important set of antecedent variables. There are many factors which affect the outcome of helping relationships, and the worker's expectations are only one of them. I do not claim they are more important than many others. But I think the evidence reviewed in these pages suggests they should never be ignored.

The debate concerning the hypothesis that professional intervention can both help and harm is reviewed. I suggest how the evidence concerning expectations may contribute to this discussion.

I will argue that the evidence presented in these pages has serious implications for members of the helping professions. The potential significance of expectations suggests that the client's *future* should be an explicit focus of the relationship. Because negative expectations could set up a harmful self-fulfilling prophecy, another change in focus is indicated for helping relationships. This involves a move from problem focused, retrospective analysis which concentrates on linking present to past pathology. In its place I suggest a more constructive problem solving which would take understanding pathology into account but go on to build a view of the client's future based upon the strengths in his personality and the more positive features of his situation.

I hope to show that it is the *behaviour* of the helping person which is the central causal factor in self-fulfilling prophecies. Thus the conclusions of this discussion reinforce the view that we should focus far more on the actual behaviour of professional helpers with clients rather than continuing to concentrate on their intellectual analysis and description of them. This view has direct implications for the selection and training of members of the helping professions.

This book is based upon my dissertation submitted for the Master's degree in Social Work at Sussex University in 1972. I should like to thank my fellow students and friends who tolerated my tendency to see self-fulfilling prophecies all round me. They gave me essential support and encouragement, particularly Caroline, who is now my wife. During this time, John Simmonds was an excellent 'model' whose expectations played an important part in what was for me a period of significant change. I should also particularly like to thank Dr Peter Mayo for the interest he has shown, both then and since, and for the invaluable suggestions he has made.

The final version of this book was made possible by the financial support of a Central Council for Education and Training in Social Work research fellowship and the Middlesex Probation and After-Care Service who allowed me leave of absence. I am indebted to my colleagues in the Probation Service, particularly those at the Tottenham Office.

Useful suggestions and feedback came from several friends and colleagues who spent considerable time reading the manuscript, particularly Robert Harris, Dr Peter Mayo, Jack Lyons and Jean Carter. I should also like to thank Professor Noel Timms for the encouragement and useful suggestions he has given me. Finally, I thank Jill Smale whose patience, perseverance and skill in typing several versions of this book have been invaluable.

This book is the product of my interaction with many people, many of whom I have only met via the written page. However, the final responsibility for the interpretations made and conclusions drawn from these transactions, and written in these pages, rests with me.

Chapter one

Introduction

The literature of the helping professions contains more than its fair share of panaceas and schools of thought. Psychologically orientated caseworkers battle with politically minded community workers, while behaviour therapists fight it out with psychoanalysts. Radical therapists challenge them all. An outsider might conclude that there is a competition to help an acute shortage of clients.

The grand synthesis or even a categorisation of who and what is effective with whom has yet to be accomplished. There are signs that some of these differences are being bridged but much more needs to be done.

Writers do not always intend to offer their theories as panaceas. But overstressed workers pressed by answer-seeking clients seize upon the writings of innovators as solutions to problems far beyond the range offered by their instigators. Thus family therapy is put forward as a solution for what is a problem of poor housing, and re-allocation of material resources suggested to overcome those inter-personal difficulties that are suffered by both rich and poor. It is not just that assessment of need is faulty but often that training in a 'school' of help means that the helper has only one solution to offer.

This book does not offer a panacea nor is it an attempt to suggest how change can or should be brought about in clients or their environments. The central argument is that the expectations of the professional helping person will tend to act as a self-fulfilling prophecy and thus affect the outcome of his efforts. These expectations are but one of a series of variables which influence change and so their effect should not be exaggerated. But if the hypothesis is proved then their potential influence cannot be overlooked. The evidence presented will suggest that these expectations may be a significant factor in professional intervention being harmful as well as helpful to clients. Although it will be shown that expectations can be crucial to outcome it is not suggested that if the expectations are right everything else will follow. But the reader might conclude that if expectations are not right the client is best left alone.

The controversy over the efficacy of psychotherapy, casework and counselling has brought into the open other indications that professional helpers can be harmful as well as helpful and this subject will be fully reviewed in the course of the discussion.

The conclusions of this debate have important implications for practice. It will be argued, for instance, that pathology-focused retrospective analysis, typified by psychoanalysis, can have dangers and that there is a need to bring the future into the focus of intervention and to pay more than lip service to the strengths of clients. The need to focus on the actual behaviour of professional helpers as opposed to the present emphasis on their academic training, and intellectual interpretations of events, will also be underlined.

The need for a new theoretical framework

It would be usual to begin our discussion by defining the types of professional-helping relationships which are central to this book i.e. psychotherapy, social casework and counselling. However, instead of doing so it is proposed that we illustrate the theoretical framework within which we will work by challenging the use of these nebulous yet all-embracing concepts.

Psychotherapy, casework, counselling are terms which like 'the ether' have been used to cover many things and describe a large number of divergent and often apparently

conflicting theories. Psychotherapy, for example, encom-
passes Krasner's behaviour theory-based 'reinforcement
machine' on the one hand (Krasner, 1962), and Rogers'
accepting, empathising, congruent persons on the other
(Rogers, 1966, etc.). Casework can include a multitude of
actions (and sins) from giving money to the needy to
intensive, psychoanalytically orientated marital analysis.

To date these umbrella terms have inspired a growing
body of research literature concerning the efficacy of treatment and the pre-requisites of success. However, we should
ask; what have researchers really been studying? Often the
aims of research have been to demonstrate the superiority of
one school of therapy over another. But, since Eysenck's
first article (1952), which claimed that psychotherapy and
counselling were no more effective than 'spontaneous
remission', there has been a more concerted effort to show
that therapy *per se* is helpful.

However, Eysenck's attack, and often the defences put
forward, are in essence inappropriate because psychotherapy, etc. can hardly be considered a unitary phenomenon. It has been pointed out that to ask the question 'is
psychotherapy therapeutic?' and then go about answering
the question in the traditional way, is very much like the
medical profession testing the efficacy of drugs by randomly
giving unknown kinds of drugs in unknown quantities to
one group of patients with various complaints and no drugs
to another similar group (Truax and Carkhuff, 1964).

The efficacy of treatment debate, discussed in detail later,
has led to attempts to identify the important helpful factors
in all forms of therapy. Let us look at some of the basic
arguments which support this 'non-school' approach to
identify so called 'non-specific' therapeutic factors.

It has been traditionally assumed that the type of therapy
offered to a client is dependent upon the theoretical
orientation of the therapist but this is now open to serious
doubt. It is, indeed, somewhat ironic that this assumption
concerning theoretical orientation is made when often the
theories illustrate that the client's behaviour is dependent

upon more than his intellectual knowledge and not likely to be changed by rational argument.

Fiedler and Strupp indicate that experience is more relevant to the therapist's ability to provide the 'quality of relationship' that was successful, than the 'school' he belonged to (Fiedler, 1950, 1953; Strupp, 1962). Betz found that the crucial determinants of therapeutic outcome lay in the personal qualities of the physician not his theory (Betz, 1962). Truax and Carkhuff formed similar views during their Wisconsin and Kentucky research projects. They point out that after reading the theoretical and clinical writings of a number of fairly well-known clinicians and then listening to a psychotherapy session with a live patient, they were often struck by the vast inconsistencies between the actual practice and what was preached (Truax and Carkhuff, 1964). Wrenn demonstrated this phenomenon when he asked fifty-four counsellors to write responses to standard therapy situations which were designed to maximise theoretical differences in the way they might be handled; no relationship between their actual situational responses and their professed theoretical orientation was found (Wrenn, 1960). Egan, in a recent review of the literature in this area, concludes that there is often a gap between the practitioners' theoretical stance and practice, that practitioners with the same theoretical outlook can look quite different in practice and that helpers, who have been judged effective yet hold different theories, often look similar in practice (Egan, 1975).

The extensive research work of Truax and Carkhuff *et al.* clearly indicates that it is the interpersonal *'behaviour'* of the therapist that is important. It would seem, however, that this 'behaviour' is not directly related to the therapists' theoretical orientation but to other factors. Indeed, it has been indicated that non-professional helpers may be just as effective as professionals (Truax and Carkhuff, 1967; Carkhuff, 1969, 1971; Goldstein, 1973; Egan, 1975).

Truax and Mitchell sum up their conclusions as follows:

(1) the therapeutic endeavour is, on the average, quite ineffective; (2) counselling or therapy itself is a nonunitary phenomenon; (3) some counsellors and therapists are significantly helpful, while others are significantly harmful, with a resulting average helpfulness not demonstrably better than the average of non-professional help; (4) through close examination of existing theories and clinical writings, it is possible to identify therapeutic ingredients likely to lead to helpful and to harmful client outcomes, and, through research, to identify such ingredients; (5) it is possible to translate the research findings into training and practice; and (6) it is therefore possible to markedly enhance the average effectiveness of counselling and psychotherapy by increasing the number of psychonoxious or harmful practitioners (Truax and Mitchell, 1971, p. 301).

Jerome Frank, in his analysis of comparative healing methods, including psychotherapy, has also shown the value of identifying the common characteristics which bring about change. He shows how pre-scientific healing rituals and mythical remedies have certain essential similarities to modern healing techniques. Other writers have also emphasised the importance of this approach (Ehrenwald, 1966; Kiev, 1966; Calestro, 1972; Frank, 1973). It is now accepted in much of the literature that the study of these so-called non-specific factors affecting outcome of the helping process are as important as the specific issues identified by the various schools of thought (Strupp, 1970, 1973).

Core themes in helping relationships

I propose to break down the constructs psychotherapy, casework and counselling into their component variables, thus taking this non-school, non-specific approach further.

One of the common fundamental central themes which runs through psychotherapy, casework and counselling is that they are all, however defined, processes where the

5

interaction between people is designed to effect change, primarily in the person or people whom we shall refer to as clients. Responsibility for the relationship, and the planning or designing of how 'change' will be achieved, is invested in the person who is officially employed as the agent of change, whom we shall refer to as the professional helper.

I am very conscious of the inadequacy of the terms used throughout this discussion. To my knowledge there are no satisfactory generic terms for either the people (i.e. social workers, psychotherapists, clinical psychologists, counsellors, experimenters, doctors, hypnotists on the one hand, and clients, patients, experimentees or subjects on the other), or the process (i.e. therapy, casework, etc.). The terms 'helper' and 'helpee' have been used in the literature but are sometimes considered unsatisfactory for their somewhat patronising implications. 'Change agent' is often thought to sound too mechanistic. Perhaps the reader will bear with me then, and not hold the use of any one of these terms to be specific to a particular caste of helping professional, just as therapy will be used as a shorthand for the interaction between worker and client without necessarily being related to a medical model of help.

But to return to our discussion of the fundamentals of helping relationships. Carl Rogers has defined the helping relationship as follows:

> A relationship in which at least one of the parties has the intent of promoting the growth, development, maturity, improved functioning, improved coping with life of the other. The other in this sense, may be one individual or a group. To put it in another way, a helping relationship might be defined as one in which one of the participants intends that there should come about, in one or both parties, more appreciation of, more expression of, more functional use of the latent inner resources of the individual (Rogers, 1961, p. 40).

Thus our approach emphasises the factors which the participants bring to the arena where change is expected to take place. This arena might be the office of the social worker or the psychotherapist, the family interview, the group, the community worker's neighbourhood meeting, etc., etc. However, the scope of the evidence presented here is predominantly that which is deduced from one-to-one situations. Much of what is said is generally relevant to family and group situations, indeed to any situation where a professional worker sets out to bring about change with other people through his interaction with them. Thus the analysis applies to the change process at this fundamental level, and umbrella terms such as casework, psychotherapy, counselling, etc. can be left aside.

Later in our discussion it will be seen that another central common theme of helping relationships, introduced here, is relevant. It seems that if we look at the range of work which social workers, psychotherapists, counsellors and other helpers do, we can see much of it in terms of offering, providing, or, trying to find with the client an alternative *modus operandi*.

These alternatives may concern relatively small aspects of the client's life such as new accommodation, provision of physical aids, a change in one aspect of the client's behaviour, right up to alternative life styles such as in the case of drug addicts. On another, obviously interrelated continuum the alternative may be external, i.e. change in environment, or internal, i.e. change in the way the client views the world. Different workers in different settings will offer alternatives appropriate to their particular agency. However, I suggest that a core activity of all change agents, be they doctors, social workers, teachers or friends is to offer the client some alternative to his present situation.

Variables affecting change

The next step is to identify what types of variables exist in this process of change. So far we have referred to one set of antecedent variables, i.e. those concerning the therapist, but these are only one part of this picture.

Introduction

In any process of change there are antecedent variables which are a pre-requisite or cause of certain functionally related consequent variables. There may also be present 'intervening' variables (or catalysts) which enable the functional relationship to proceed. In terms of the helping relationship referred to above it is suggested that certain antecedent variables (the accurate empathy, genuineness and non-possessive warmth of the therapist) enable the change process to take place producing the consequent variables—'client improvement'. As yet the details of the functional relationship between these two sets of variables is vague.

The types of variables which may be fitted into this type of model are:

(1) Antecedent variables

Therapist variables: such as personality characteristics, expectancies, attitudes, theoretical orientation, training, sex, social prestige of role, etc. (see Truax and Mitchell, 1971).

Subject variables: personality characteristics, symptomatology, length of duration of 'problem', expectations and attitudes, social class, etc. (see Garfield, 1971).

Interactional variables: the actual behaviour of therapist and subject in interaction, the roles adopted by both, non-verbal communication, the tone of voice used by the therapist, i.e. the therapist's actual communication with the client and the client's responses.

Situational variables: individual, group, family, client network involvement, etc., client pre-training for therapy, length of therapy, concurrent crisis and circumstances, etc.

(2) *Intervening variables*

There will be factors such as the supportiveness of the client's network of friends and/or relatives, the social/economic resources available, etc. (where changes in these factors are not specific goals of the helping relationship).

(3) *Consequent variables*

This is the outcome of therapy—its effects for better or for worse. Measurement of 'outcome' is a major area of controversy in research into the helping process (Truax and Carkhuff, 1967; Bergin, 1971; Bergin and Strupp, 1972). We might also note that the type of alternative offered the client will be a consequent variable.

Toward an eclectic framework

The above list of variables is by no means intended to be exhaustive but merely an illustration of the type of factors involved. Our knowledge of the helping relationship is such that we can only begin to fill in this type of model of the process of change.

Because change brought about as the result of interaction between people is the central focus, this model is not restricted to research under the heading of psychotherapy, casework, etc. Thus it is proposed to inform our discussion by looking at empirical evidence from other relationships where change is the product of interaction, namely the fields of placebo medicine, experimenter bias and comparative healing. However, our purpose in looking at these areas marks a departure from the traditional focus of the literature. Placebos and experimenter bias have always been seen as 'artifacts' in behavioural research, as such the purpose of much of the research on them is to eradicate their effect. We are looking at their effect with the opposite aim in mind. It is hoped that we might understand the mechanisms involved and the light they throw on the interactional process *so as to maximise* (*not minimise*) *their effect and thus the change brought about.*

Having stressed the importance of the interaction between professional worker and client it follows that the behaviour determining characteristics of the change agent are of crucial importance. *Interaction* is after all the reciprocal behaviour of the participant individuals.

Some of the areas of research which indicate the importance of the professional's behaviour have already been referred to and it will be a recurring theme throughout the book. The antecedent variables to this behaviour inevitably involve the professional as a person, as Truax and Mitchell explain:

> Research efforts to isolate variables in the therapeutic
> process that effectively alter maladaptive behaviour
> must involve the PERSON of the therapist. Whether we
> call him a therapist, a counselor, a doctor, a social
> worker, a priest, an educator, or simply a 'helping
> person' he is officially employed as the agent or catalyst
> for change. Effective implementation of specific
> techniques must rest on his personal qualities. He is
> basic to the psychosocial endeavour to change the
> patient FOR THE BETTER. . . . Much emphasis is
> given to particular techniques or procedures that are
> useful for inducing positive behavioural change in
> people. These techniques and procedures do not occur
> in pure form, but instead are grafted onto the existing
> qualities of the human being who serves as a change
> agent (Truax and Mitchell, 1971, p. 299).

As the central hypothesis of the book is supported by more and more evidence the importance of this approach will be underlined. It is not suggested that the intellectual development of the change agent should be ignored but it is necessary for this development to have a *practical impact* on his ability to help (see Egan, 1975).

For a complete view of the helping process it would be necessary to analyse all the variables connected with the change process but this is beyond the scope of this book. Here it is proposed to focus on the change agent's expectations of the outcome of therapy and his client's future behaviour, and to test against a review of the available relevant evidence the hypothesis already stated, i.e. that the expectations of the helping person tend to act as a self-fulfilling prophecy and thus affect the outcome of his efforts.

The expectations of the change agent have been chosen because it seems to me that the future of the client is often ignored when his problems are discussed. Much emphasis has been placed on the client's past. It is perhaps as a result of the helping profession's felt need for scientific respectability that predominantly they cling to explanations of their client's problems that rest on 'evidence'. This sort of 'evidence' can only be found in the past. But some writers have indicated the need to look beyond it.

G. A. Kelly (1955) has claimed that much of man's behaviour is determined by his expectations, which will be constantly reviewed and modified. Rychlak (1968) points out that the existence of 'mind' in man cannot be ignored and that concepts of mentality demand the use of a final cause construct by which he means 'for the sake of something'. Jerome Frank (1968, 1973) has argued for the importance of hope in healing, indicating its major significance as an important client and therapist antecedent variable. This view will be discussed in more detail later.

Adler and then Jung came into conflict with Freud's determinism and stressed the importance of man's view of the future, his ideals and goals. Jung was aware not only of the need to take the future into account but also of the scientific difficulties of doing so. Thus he wrote in 1916 when distinguishing his analytical psychology from Freudian psychoanalysis:

> The Zurich School has in view the end-result of analysis, and it regards the fundamental thoughts and impulses of the unconscious as symbols, indicative of a definite

line of future development. We must admit, however, that there is *no scientific justification* for such a procedure, because our present-day science is based wholly on causality. But causality is only one principle, and psychology cannot be exhausted by causal method only, because the mind lives by aims as well (original italics, Jung, 1961, p. 292).

Preview of discussion

The presentation of the evidence begins in the next chapter with a description of the self-fulfilling prophecy distinguishing it from accurate prophecy and other concepts used in the literature such as prognostic expectations. The use of the concept is then extended by breaking it down into its three component parts; the prediction, behaviour based on the prediction and outcome caused by the behaviour. The similarities between this approach and others, particularly labelling theory, will then be discussed.

Chapter 3 is a review of the major indirect areas of artifact research, which provide evidence that the expectations of the professional, in these cases the researcher, the hypnotist and the medical experimenter, affect the outcome of their contact with their clients and demonstrate how this influence can be better understood by applying the self-fulfilling prophecy model previously defined. It will be shown that these expectations can precipitate a variety of outcomes which might be judged as for better or for worse.

The fourth chapter opens by linking the placebo effects already described to helping relationships designed to bring about change and by exploring the role of hope and faith in the process of healing and change. The main task is to review the direct research evidence, psychotherapy research, which demonstrates the significance of expectations in helping relationships. At this stage it can be concluded that the evidence supports our central hypothesis that expectations are indeed an important and often crucial variable and that they may influence the interaction of the helping relationship in such a way that a self-fulfilling prophecy is set in motion. It is also shown that these processes may be overt or implicit and communicated in subtle or explicit ways and that there are limitations on the potency of the effect of expectations. The need for more specific research is highlighted.

The question is then posed; how does the self-fulfilling prophecy work in helping relationships? Chapter 5 sets out to explore this question by reviewing the evidence on prophecy communication. It will be argued that all types of intervention by professional helpers involve a degree of influence over the client. The indications are that the worker's differing expectations will lead him to display differing degrees of certain behaviour characteristics towards his clients. For example, optimism and liking leading to the worker showing more warmth. The growing body of research which indicates that these behaviour characteristics are of great significance to the outcome of helping relationships is summarised. A model for understanding the process is then suggested. In this the worker's expectations affect the interaction by causing him to behave in a way which reinforces that behaviour of the client which is in accordance with the worker's prophecy. Thus the three stages of the self-fulfilling prophecy in helping relationships are again demonstrated and analysed by reference to psychological theories which stress the importance of 'reinforcement' and 'modelling'. The need to focus on the behaviour of change agents introduced in the preceding discussions is now further underlined and it becomes clear that the variables concerning this behaviour are of crucial importance for further study.

Having established the importance of expectations and suggested how they may be communicated, the discussion in chapter 6 turns to a major approach to helping relationships, i.e. that of Client-Centred Therapy. This approach is chosen because of the degree to which client-centred therapists have concerned themselves with outcome research in attempts to demonstrate the effectiveness of intervention.

Introduction

An analysis of the basic philosophy, the behaviour advocated by these workers, and the final outcome, are reviewed as examples of the three stages of a self-fulfilling prophecy. This analysis opens up discussion about the importance of the future as a focus of the helping relationship.

The seventh chapter discusses how the potency of the change agent as prophet might be increased. By returning to the literature analysed in previous chapters it is possible to indicate how the influence of expectations may be maximised. The range and type of expectations that bring about optimum change are examined. For example, expectations that are too high tend to have no effect and in some cases may act as an 'anti-self-fulfilling prophecy' that is, a prophecy which brings about the opposite effect to that expected. It will also be seen that the prestige and status of the helper are of importance and that he is but one prophet in the client system. It should also be pointed out at this stage that in order for expectations to bring about change it must be possible for that change to be caused by the prophet's behaviour, or by the behaviour of those who come to share the prophecy. It is in this chapter that the intention is carried out to stand so called 'artifact' research on its head, that is to maximise rather than minimise the effect of these variables.

The 'for better or for worse' argument is discussed in chapter 8. The work concerning the effectiveness of casework, psychotherapy, counselling and related forms of intervention is reviewed. The more recent conclusions drawn from the evidence, that these forms of treatment may be harmful as well as helpful, are underlined. The assumption, often made by members of the helping professions, that they 'help or have no effect' is challenged. Then the preceding discussions are drawn upon to illustrate how expectations may form a significant link in this argument. That is, how positive expectations lead to self-fulfilling prophecies that help people to get better, while negative expectations operate through the same mechanism to make them worse. Thus the importance of identifying the client's strengths, and the dangers of focusing entirely on pathology are emphasised. The importance of the future as a focus of helping is further underlined. These arguments imply serious criticisms of the practices of some schools of therapy, such as Freudian psychoanalysis.

The final chapter outlines the major implications of this discussion for the practice and training of change agents in the helping professions. For example, the need to optimise the effect of expectations by matching clients to workers who will recognise their potential; the need for workers to develop awareness of and be explicit about their expectations, modifying them to a realistic level; the need to maximise the potency of the change agent as a prophet will be stressed for professional practice. Implications for training will include the necessity to focus upon the *behaviour* of the worker and not solely upon his intellectual understanding. It will be implied that further research should be focused on the moment by moment interaction between workers and clients so that we might understand the processes described here and further identify the growth-producing behaviour of professional helpers. Finally, the for better, for worse conclusions underline the need to guard against stunting and harmful expectations and the danger of focusing exclusively on the retrospective pathology of the client.

Chapter two

The self-fulfilling prophecy

Expectations, prognostic expectations and self-fulfilling prophecies

Goldstein was the first to look in detail at the importance of expectations, that is the anticipation and/or probability of things happening, in human relations. He coined the term 'Prognostic Expectations' to distinguish between a correct prognosis and those expectations which actually change what happens. He outlines his concept as follows:

> It is suggested that the obtained finding of a significant difference in therapist prognostic expectancies between improved and unimproved patients is *not* a major function of the fact that the prognosis for improved patients may possibly have been objectively good, and therefore, might have been realised in patient improvement regardless of who the psychotherapist was. It is assumed, instead, that such psychotherapist expectancies are in fact communicated to the patient, colour their interactions, influence their relationship and, thus, effect the degree of patient improvement (Goldstein, 1962, p. 39).

Thus prognostic expectations are active agents in the change process. However, these processes can be further understood if the self-fulfilling prophecy concept, introduced by the sociologist R. K. Merton, is broken down into its component parts so as to provide a model for applying to the interaction between people. This concept can best be illustrated by looking at some examples.

Merton's discussion starts with the example of 'The Last National Bank': It starts the day as a solvent institution but a rumour is spreading in the town that the bank will fail. This prophecy leads people to act, and they rush to the bank to withdraw their deposits. Until they believed the prophecy they were wrong, the bank was safe, but when they believed, and acted on their belief, the prophecy became true—the run on the bank drained its resources and the bank failed (Merton, 1948).

Allport uses the concept to attempt to understand the causes of war; although most people deplore war, they none the less *expect* it to continue and, he says, what people expect determines their behaviour. He points out how expectations feed on themselves and seek out their own reinforcement. Thus aggression breeds aggression. So the expectation that war is to be waged is communicated to the opponent-to-be who reacts by preparing for war, an act which confirms the first nation's expectation, strengthens it and leads to greater preparation for war thus setting in motion a mutually reinforcing feedback system (Allport, 1950).

These examples show the negative effect of a prophecy but it can work positively too. Take the case of 'Sweeney's miracle' for example: James Sweeney taught industrial management and psychiatry at Tulane University where he was responsible for the operation of the Biomedical Computer Center. It was Sweeney's expectation that he could make even a poorly educated negro into a computer operator. The poorly educated negro chosen was George Johnson, a former hospital porter who became janitor at the computer centre. In the morning he swept and cleaned, and in the afternoon he learned about computers. He was learning a great deal about computers when word circulated that to be a computer operator one had to earn a certain score on an IQ test. Johnson took the test, which showed that he should not even be able to learn to type, much less operate a computer. But Sweeney was not convinced. He went to the administration and threatened: no Johnson, no

17

Sweeney. Both stayed; Sweeney still runs the computer centre, and Johnson now runs the main computer room in which position he is responsible for the training of new employees.

This example shows not only that self-fulfilling prophecies can have positive results but also that the status and conviction of the prophet is important if contrary expectations—in this case the rumours and the IQ test—are not going to over-ride the potency of the original prophecy.

So far the expectations which have formed our prophecy have been fairly explicit and the process fairly public but that this need not be so is illustrated by the story of Clever Hans: Clever Hans was a horse who could add, subtract, multiply, divide, spell and read all by means of tapping his foot to signal the correct answer. However, it was found that these abilities could be explained if we looked at the person who asked the questions rather than at the horse. A psychologist, Pfungst, carried out a series of experiments in which he discovered that Hans could only answer questions if the questioner himself knew the answer and was visible to the horse during his foot-tapping of the solution. It was found that whenever people asked Hans a question they leaned forward very slightly to see Hans' hoof. This, unintentionally, was the signal that started Hans tapping. Then as Hans approached the number of taps representing the right answer the questioners would typically show a tiny head movement—this was the signal for Hans to stop and demonstrate the right answer again. The questioner by expecting Hans to stop at the right answer was actually 'telling' him the right answer and thereby fulfilling his own prophecy. Pfungst also added to the understanding of this phenomenon by showing that the questioners were not equally good at giving the cues to obtain the correct responses. He found that among the characteristics of the more successful unintentional influencers were those of tact, an air of dominance, attention to the business at hand, and a facility for motor discharge (Pfungst, 1911).

These four examples of the self-fulfilling prophecy all

demonstrate the central characteristics of the concept. The first essential feature is that outlined by Goldstein in defining prognostic expectations, i.e. that prognostic expectations, and we now include self-fulfilling prophecies, are distinct from a prognosis or a non-self-fulfilling prophecy in as much as without the expectation being formed or stated, the forecasted outcome would not have come about: the bank would not have failed, Johnson would have remained a janitor, Clever Hans would only be able to tap at random, etc.

The three stages of the self-fulfilling prophecy

Merton claims that essentially the self-fulfilling prophecy is false. Yet by definition a self-fulfilling prophecy is true, that is to say when assessed in retrospect we find that the prophesied event or condition has come about. It is not possible to assess the validity of prediction until time has passed. So we must take it that the crucial, identifying feature which makes an expectation self-fulfilling is that the result would not have come about without the intervention of the prophecy. We can carry our analysis of the mechanism one stage further by reflecting back over our examples. We see that essentially each of these self-fulfilling prophecies has three stages: first the prediction is formed; action and subsequent behaviour are then taken as a result of this prediction; this behaviour then brings about the prophesied event or behaviour. Thus, we can break down the concept of the self-fulfilling prophecy into these three essential stages.

Table 1 is designed to show these stages, admittedly in an over-simplified form, in order to demonstrate their causal relationship.

If we take this model we can see that it is the *behaviour,* based on the prophecy, which causes the crucial difference between a self-fulfilling prophecy and a prophecy which is not *self*-fulfilling; it is the *behaviour* of the therapist which is the difference between a prognosis and prognostic expectations. An essential feature of this *behaviour* is that it is an *active* intervention, whether deliberately planned or not.

19

The self-fulfilling prophecy

TABLE 1 The three stages of the self-fulfilling prophecy as illustrated by the examples given

Stage One Expectation and prediction	Stage Two Behaviour based on Stage One	Stage Three The consequences of the behaviour in Stage Two
Prophecy	Behaviour	The prophecy fulfilled
1. The bank will fail.	Withdrawal of money; drying up of resources.	The bank fails due to lack of funds.
2. The 'enemy' will fight.	Both sides arm and are defensively hostile.	Hostility finally breaks out and the arms are used.
3. Johnson can learn to operate a computer.	Sweeney teaches him and overcomes opposition.	Johnson runs the computer room.
4. Clever Hans can count (etc.).	Move to watch Hans tap, move when Hans should stop.	Hans counts the right number, i.e. taps when signalled to start and finish.

Characteristics of self-fulfilling prophecies

From our examples we can also tentatively suggest some more specific characteristics of self-fulfilling prophecies. First, they can work in any direction, either for better (improvement), or for worse (deterioration). Second they can be conscious or unconscious, implicit or explicit; they may come about in a fairly public, open way or as a subtle, hidden mechanism. Allport's example shows us how they may have a reciprocal nature—setting in motion a mutually reinforcing feedback system. Finally, the status and characteristics of the prophet seem to be important variables in the potency of the prophecy.

At this point we should note that the relationship between prophecy and outcome is not always clear-cut and direct. For example, Merton talked of the 'suicidal prophecy' which is one which predicts its own opposite (Merton, 1948). We may illustrate this type of anti-self-fulfilling prophecy by looking at the anxious doctor who, having prophesied his patient's imminent death, takes extraordinarily good care of him and actually the patient improves.

However, in this last example as in those above we see that it is the behaviour precipitated by the prophecy which is the crucial variable. It is this focus on behaviour which may enable us to overcome a crucial difficulty in understanding research in this area; can you distinguish between a prophecy actually being correct, that is, based on accurate information and subsequently proved by time, and a situation which has come about by a self-fulfilling prophecy? We can answer this question by referring to the three stages which we identified above. If we can show that the end result is causally linked (in part or in total) to the behaviour which was precipitated by the prophecy, then we can accurately analyse the situation as a self-fulfilling prophecy. To put this another way—a self-fulfilling prophecy has occurred when it has been shown that the 'intervention' of the prophecy/prophet was a causal link in the chain of events leading to the prophesied outcome. The accurate/correct prophecy by contrast requires no such intervention.

Self-fulfilling prophecies and labelling theory

The self-fulfilling prophecy mechanism has close parallels with the labelling theory of deviancy and mental illness. It is not proposed to go into this area in depth here. It will, however, probably prove useful to outline the fundamental position of the labelling theorists, and indicate the interconnection between that theory and the central hypothesis and evidence presented in this book. It should be said that our interest in labelling theory at this stage is primarily as a description of certain processes within society. It is not my intention to advocate its ideology or argue its cause as a theory of deviancy.

The basic position of the labelling theorists is that deviance is created by society. By this they do not mean that the causes of deviance are located in the social situation of

21

the deviant or in 'social factors' which prompt his action. What they mean is that social groups create deviance by making the rules whose infraction constitutes deviance, and by applying those rules to particular people, and labelling them outsiders. From this point of view, deviance is *not* a quality of the act the person commits, but rather a consequence of the application by others of rules and sanctions to an 'offender'. Thus the deviant is one to whom that label has successfully been applied and deviant behaviour is that behaviour which people so label (Becker, 1963). The theory also denies that deviancy arises out of the individual's personality. But rather claims that the label is likely to be incorporated into the deviant's own self-definition and in that way be implanted in the personality by others, that is labellers (Hardiker, 1972).

This view of deviant behaviour can be illustrated by comparing the activities of the drug pusher and the grocery wholesaler. Essentially the behaviour of the two is the same; both seek out their sources of supply and sale and carry out their transactions at both ends in order to make a personal profit. But one is 'deviant', the other 'legitimate' because of the way in which society at large views the commodity being bought and sold. I am not suggesting for a moment that the drug pusher is really, or should be considered, legitimate but merely indicating that it is not his behaviour *per se* which is deviant. It should be pointed out that in later writings these theorists have been keen to explain that labelling theory does not claim to offer a solution to the problem of what *causes* deviant behaviour. Its aim is to enlarge the area taken into consideration in the study of deviancy by including the activities of others than the allegedly deviant actor (Becker, 1973; Scheff, 1975).

However, what they do claim is that labelling places the actor in circumstances which make it harder for him to continue the normal routines of life and so he is provoked into further 'abnormal' actions. An obvious example is when a prison or psychiatric record makes it harder for a person to find 'respectable' employment. This is best understood by the concept of the deviant career (Becker, 1963; Rubington and Weinberg, 1973). This concept points out how becoming an 'outsider' results from a sequence of events and is not wholly dependent upon a 'deviant' act and its causes. The first stage is the commission of a non-conforming act. For the 'deviant career' to proceed it is necessary for the actor to be identified, i.e. caught, and publicly labelled. The next stage, and it is here that the self-fulfilling prophecy comes in, is a result of people's reaction to the label.

Of course many, if not all, people commit non-conforming acts without becoming outsiders. Becker points out that the deviant label has to assume a 'master status'. i.e. that by which the person is most readily identified. He goes on to describe the consequences:

> Treating a person as though he were generally rather than specifically deviant produces a self-fulfilling prophecy. It sets in motion several mechanisms which conspire to shape the person in the image people have of him. In the first place one tends to be cut off, after being identified as deviant, from participation in more conventional groups, even though the specific consequences of the particular deviant activity might never of themselves have caused the isolation had there not also been the public knowledge and reaction to it. For example, being a homosexual may not affect one's ability to do office work, but to be known as a homosexual in an office may make it impossible to continue working there (Becker, 1963, p. 34).

Now the model of the self-fulfilling prophecy described above draws out the need to see clearly that if the process described is to take place it is because the label causes people to make predictions about the actor's future behaviour. Their behaviour toward the actor is based on these predictions and it is this behaviour rather than the label *per se* which may precipitate further deviant behaviour.

The final stages of a deviant career are reached when the

23

actor identifies with and joins a deviant sub-group which reinforces his own identity and legitimises it amongst his peers. It now only remains for him fully to accept and present a deviant identity.

Thus the labelling theory model is one where a succession of precipitating factors have to be negotiated by the actor and contribute to him becoming an 'outsider'. At any of these stages circumstances, for example the behaviour of the actor, other people's reaction to it and the actor's subsequent reaction to their reaction, may or may not combine in a way which precipitates the continuation of that career (Rubington and Weinberg, 1973).

It can be seen from the above discussion that a central issue in the theory is whether in fact the effect of labelling can be to precipitate further deviant behaviour in the person so labelled. It is therefore apparent that the discussion of our central hypothesis is directly relevant to the process described by the labelling theorists and that within that model the professional helper might play a significant part in furthering or diverting a deviant career.

However, the evidence presented by labelling theorists is sparse and often of a general, descriptive nature; Scheff points out that up to 1975 there were eighteen studies related explicitly to labelling theory available, of which thirteen support the theory, but five fail to do so (Scheff, 1975). If, in our subsequent discussion, the evidence supports the view that people's expectations can indeed work as self-fulfilling prophecies and thus affect other people's behaviour, then we will have confirmed that the type of social phenomenon described by the labelling theorists is indeed possible. If, that is, the act of labelling involves a prediction about future behaviour.

Chapter three

Bias, hypnosis and placebos

The areas of artifact and hypnosis research provide evidence that expectations can precipitate change. The deliberate use of procedures for which we have no direct scientific causal explanation, that is placebos and other artifacts, sometimes arouses controversy and suggestions of quackery. However, I think that close scrutiny of the evidence may sufficiently demystify these mechanisms for them to be considered legitimate. The aim is to show that the evidence supports the hypothesis that expectations can influence the interaction of the relationship between people in such a way that self-fulfilling prophecy mechanisms are set in motion. This leads on to standing artifact research on its head by asking, how can we maximise their effect instead of the more usual aim of minimising or eradicating their power?

Experimenter and teacher bias

Robert Rosenthal's work has highlighted the effect of experimenter bias and subsequently related this to the self-fulfilling prophecy (Rosenthal, 1966; Rosenthal and Jacobson, 1968; Rosenthal, 1969). In his now famous rat-learning study Rosenthal demonstrated that experimenters obtained the results they wanted or expected. His experimenters were led to believe that their rats were genetically determined to be 'bright' or 'dull', although, in fact, both sets of rats were all from the same strain. Experimenters expecting their rats to be bright obtained

25

significantly better learning results than those expecting their rats to be dull. This experiment is supported by over twenty others involving several hundred rats and planaria and many experimenters (Rosenthal, 1966).

It would seem then that we have the first and third stages of a self-fulfilling prophecy. The second is completed when we consider Rosenthal's comments on the experimenters whose rats learned more, as opposed to those who had dull rats. The first viewed their animals as brighter, more pleasant and more likeable than did the latter. They felt more relaxed when handling the animals and described their behaviour toward them as more pleasant, friendly, enthusiastic and less talkative. They also handled the rats more often and more gently (Rosenthal, 1966). Although this does not provide definite evidence of a causal link it does indicate that the difference in the samples is not just the initial expectation. This link will be discussed later when we consider how expectations are communicated.

Rosenthal also found that experimenter bias worked with human subjects rating photographs of people for success or failure. The results showed clearly that every experimenter who had been led to expect ratings of people as successful obtained a higher average rating of success than did any experimenter expecting ratings of people less successful. These findings have been replicated in further studies (Rosenthal, 1966).

We should note that the experimenter's expectations do not always seem to affect his results. Although the reasons for these 'failures' are not clear from the studies, they may be consistent with our hypothesis in as much as it may be that, in these instances, the expectations failed to produce the prophecy fulfilling behaviour. Indeed, further research in this programme showed that the bias effect was not constant but could be varied by other factors. It was found, for example, that subjects' expectations of the experimenter's appropriate role behaviour influenced the effect of bias. Early results of research can determine the performance of the experimenter and thus subsequent results, presumably by a reinforcement type principle. It was also found that too large or too obvious an incentive to affect the results of research *diminished* the experimenter bias effect. Motivation and non-specific factors such as greeting, seating and instructions given were found to be significant as were the types of verbal and visual cues given. The prestige of the experimenter was found to be significant as were his likeability, personality, warmth and interest in the subject (Rosenthal, 1966, 1969).

Rosenthal translated and tested his view that one person's expectation of another's behaviour could come to serve as a self-fulfilling prophecy, in his now famous experiments at Oak School. This research provides important evidence that the mechanism can potentially be transferred from the laboratory to a real life situation and still show its potency (Rosenthal and Jacobson, 1968). In this experiment teachers were led to expect an increase in the performance of some of their pupils who had actually been picked at random. The children in the school were tested at the beginning of the year, at the end of one semester, after a full academic year, and after two full academic years. Expectancy advantage was defined by the degree to which IQ gains by the 'special' children exceeded the average gains of the rest of the children. Rosenthal and Jacobson found that after the first year of the experiment a significant expectancy advantage existed, and that it was especially great among children of the first and second grades. The advantage of having been expected to bloom was evident for these younger children in total IQ, verbal IQ, and reasoning IQ. The control-group children of these grades gained well in IQ, 19 per cent of them gaining twenty or more total IQ points. The 'special' children, however, showed 47 per cent of their number gaining twenty or more total IQ points.

The experimenters go on to qualify this statement in accordance to the subsequent testing and specific conditions at the school, but it seems clear that the prophecy fed to the teachers at the beginning of the experiment did, indeed, have a self-fulfilling affect, i.e. the predicted improvement was seen in the children after a period of time, despite no 'real' grounds for expecting this at the beginning of the experiment. The experimenters speculate that teachers tended to behave differently to the 'special' children and maybe thus have communicated their expectations (Rosenthal and Jacobson, 1968).

Rosenthal has warned that the effects of experimenter's expectations are found most often in studies of animal learning, laboratory interviews, inkblot tests and reaction time. They are found least often in studies of psychologic-physical judgments and person perception, and about half the time in studies of human learning and ability (Rosenthal, 1969).

None the less, the Oak School experiments and the so-called 'Pygmalion effect' have aroused considerable controversy. It would seem that the IQ tests used were not very satisfactory and that the statistical analysis of the results is open to serious criticism (Snow, 1969; Farley, 1972). However, subsequent studies have produced similar findings to those at Oak School. In one of these it was found that induced high expectations promoted an increase in performance, as measured on objective tests, in institutionalised, adolescent female offenders. Improvement in their classroom behaviour was also observed (Meichenbaum, Bowers and Ross, 1969). Consistent findings were found amongst college students while another study found similar results when the students themselves were directly informed that they were 'late bloomers' (Rubovits and Maehr, 1971; Meichenbaum and Smart, 1971). There have been other studies which replicate these findings (see Krasner and Ullman, 1973). Therefore, on balance it would seem that the 'Pygmalion effect' does indeed exist.

Rosenthal's approach to this topic is essentially different from the analysis of the self-fulfilling prophecy outlined in the previous chapter. In that it was noted that the middle stage, that is behaviour based on prophecy which causes the prophesied outcome, was necessary to show that an expectation was self-fulfilling as opposed to accurate. In the above experiments a general design was used involving two groups of subjects about one of whom the teachers or experimenters were fed expectations which were not based on their own observations. Thus, as the whole situation for both groups has been experimentally manipulated, the potency of expectation can be deduced because it is the only different variable in the two groups studied. The middle stage of our model of the self-fulfilling prophecy is considered separately under the heading of the communication of prophecy and will be discussed in more detail in chapter 5.

Hypnosis

The next area of research reviewed, hypnosis, also provides evidence that one person's expectations can influence the behaviour of another, in as much as the hypnotist's suggestions are promoted by his own expectations that the subject will respond.

Research in this area has indicated that people can be responsive to the expectancies of the experimenter while still maintaining that the 'hypnotic state' is a special category of consciousness (Orne, 1962; Orne and Schribe, 1964). However, Barber has now pointed out that the 'hypnotic state' assumptions are entangled in tautological reasoning; that the presumed hypnotic state is directly or indirectly inferred from responses to suggestions and is then used circularly to account for responses to suggestions. The central hypothesis of his argument is that it is unnecessary and unparsimonious to postulate a 'hypnotic state of consciousness' to explain responses to suggestions of muscular rigidities, analgesia, age regressions, hallucination, amnesia and so on. By a series of experiments he shows how the symptoms of presumed hypnotic states are products of the behaviour in the interaction between experimenter and subject, and the various antecedent variables both bring to the situation (Barber, 1969).

The mechanisms at work in the situations described can be looked at in terms of the self-fulfilling prophecy model.

In doing so we are extending our use of the concept, as applied to Rosenthal's work, by introducing the inter-relationship of the expectations of both the experimenters (professionals) and the subjects (clients) into the situation. Barber summarises the 'hypnotic process' as containing four sets of antecedent variables:

1) A set of subject variables such as subjects' attitudes and expectancies with respect to the test situation.
2) A set of procedural variables such as the specific wording of the test-suggestions, the tone of voice, pitch and inflections used in presenting the test suggestions, and the specific wording and tone of the questions used to elicit subjective reports.
3) A second set of procedural variables that are commonly subsumed under the label of *hypnotic induction procedure* such as statements which define the situation as 'hypnosis', motivational instructions, and repetitive suggestions of relaxation, drowsiness and sleep.
4) A set of experimenter variables such as experimenter's attitudes expectancies, and 'biases' (Barber, 1969, pp. 227-8).

Reflection on these variables reveals that they can be matched to the self-fulfilling prophecy model. Sets one and four incorporate the prophecies of experimenter and subject. The second behaviour stage of the self-fulfilling prophecy model is outlined in the second and third set of variables outlined above. Barber has shown in his experiments that the result of the interaction of these variables at optimum levels is behaviour often ascribed to 'hypnotic' states, whether a 'hypnotic state of consciousness' is assumed or not. This then completes the third stage of the self-fulfilling prophecy.

Barber's research findings and the importance of expectations can be illustrated from a couple of examples. First by applying hypnotic procedures to a sample of children he discovered that those who did not know what hypnotic behaviour was could not be 'hypnotised'. That is, not knowing what to expect they did not know how to perform as if hypnotised. Second, he studied the phenomena of 'age regression' under 'hypnosis' and demonstrated that the relevant variables were related to the expectations and behaviour of the experimenter. If he behaved towards suggestible clients in an 'adult to child' way then so-called age regression resulted (Barber, 1969).

There are, of course, many experimenters and practitioners in the field of hypnosis who do not subscribe to the 'non-state' theory (Hilgard, 1973). But many of the critics of Barber's work have been answered and Krasner and Ullman conclude their summary of the evidence by pointing out that although the 'hypnotic trance state' may not be disproved it is more likely to be found eventually to be unnecessary in explaining the behaviour involved (Chaves, 1968; Krasner and Ullman, 1973). However, there is a strong consensus amongst both 'state' and 'non-state' theorists on the relevance and power of suggestion and expectations in the process which is the central concern of our discussion (Spanos and Barber, 1974).

It is not claimed that hypnosis is simply the product of a self-fulfilling prophecy—there are a series of other variables which are significant. It is, however, claimed that both experimenter and subject expectations are one set of variables which influence behaviour in such a way as to bring about a self-fulfilling prophecy. Barber's work links with and confirms that of Rosenthal on experimenter bias. Barber writes:

> It is clear that with few exceptions investigators working in this area have had very strong 'expectancy bias'. For instance, with few exceptions, investigators have expected more dramatic or 'better' results with 'hypnotized' subjects than 'awake' subjects. In some studies these expectancies were apparently so strong that a waking comparison group was not used; apparently it was assumed that non-hypnotized subjects

31

could not or would not perform 'hypnotic' behaviours (Barber, 1969, p. 233).

The effects of 'hypnosis' and experimenter bias are normally short-lived. The 'Pygmalion effect' however may be of more lasting significance as is the effect of placebos.

Placebos

A *placebo* is defined as any therapy, or that component of any therapy, that is deliberately used for its non-specific, psychophysiologic effect, or that is used for its presumed specific effect on a patient, symptom, or illness, but which unknown to patient and therapist, is without specific activity for the condition being treated. A *placebo*, when used as a control in experimental studies, is defined as a substance or procedure that is without specific activity for the condition being evaluated.

The *placebo effect* is defined as the nonspecific, psychologic, or psychophysiologic effect produced by placebos (Shapiro, 1971, p. 440).

The importance of placebos is underlined by Shapiro, whose review of prescientific medicine led him to the following conclusion:

Today we know that the effectiveness of these procedures and medications was due to psychological factors often referred to as the placebo effect. Since almost all medications until recently were placebos, the history of medical treatment can be characterised largely as the history of the placebo effect (Shapiro, 1971).

Their status in modern medicine remains one of great significance:

Placebos can be more powerful than, and reverse the action of, potent active drugs (Wolf, 1959). The incidence of placebo reactions approaches one hundred per cent in some studies. Placebos can have profound effects on organic illnesses, and possibly even on malignancies (Shapiro, 1963). Placebos can often mimic the effects of active drugs (Lasagna, Laties, and Doman, 1958). Uncontrolled studies report that drugs are effective four or five times more frequently than do controlled studies (Foulds, 1958; Fox, 1961). Placebo effects are so omnipresent that if they are not reported in controlled studies, these are commonly considered unreliable. Increased appreciation of placebo effects is reflected in the speculation that future historians will record the major medical achievement of the last decade as the development of methodology and controlled experimentation to test the efficacy of treatment (Shapiro, 1971, p. 442).

We, and others, have already made a case for looking at these areas in an attempt to understand the helping relationship (Rosenthal and Frank, 1956; Goldstein, 1962; Krasner, 1962; Ehrenwald, 1966; Frank, 1973). Shapiro underlines this case:

> Let us remember that both psychotherapy and the placebo effect function solely through a psychological mechanism. Adamant claims that psychotherapy is not susceptible to placebo effects conform to the principle that every placebo once accepted was vigorously defended as a nonplacebo. Medical history clearly demonstrates that despite the sensitivity of many practitioners to the non specific or placebo effects of others, they were usually insensitive to their own. In fact, this insensitivity increases the potency of the placebo which once begun is a self-fulfilling prophecy (Shapiro, 1971).

However, it is necessary for consistency with our theoretical framework to note that Shapiro's distinction between psychotherapy relationships and relationships in which placebos are prescribed is an unnecessary one. We take the

33

view that the prescribing and taking of a placebo is part of the interaction between a professional helping person (the doctor or nurse) and his client (patient). We take Shapiro's point that 'insensitivity increasing the potency of the placebo effect' is an indication that faith and expectation of an outcome are stronger and more likely to be fulfilled if unquestioned.

Shapiro focuses on the patient-therapist relationship and its 'transference' perspectives in order to attempt to understand 'placebogenesis'. Like Jerome Frank and others he recognises the importance of the physician's role in society as healer, priest and scientist (Jung, 1933; Kiev, 1966; Ehrenwald, 1966; Calestro, 1972; Frank, 1973). He sees this, and the 'unrealistic' expectations that are aroused, as the source of the hope and optimism reflected in positive and negative placebo reactions. Freud also indicated that prescientific therapies and the healers of the day were effective because 'In order to effect a cure a condition of "expectant faith" was induced in the sick person, the same condition which answers a similar purpose for us today' (Freud, 1904, quoted p. 173, Kiev, 1966).

In order to understand these relationships further Shapiro analyses the relevant patient, situation and physician variables as indicated by research, concluding that the therapist's interest in the patient, treatment and results is related to success in treatment and placebo effects. He also concludes that there is a complex interaction between therapist's interest in the patient, the treatment, and the ultimate results; and that the understanding of the complex interactions of the therapist's interest in the patient, treatment and results requires more than retrospective speculation (Shapiro, 1971). This last expression of the need for further research into the mechanisms involved indicates that at present our understanding of the precise nature of placebogenesis is far from complete.

There are many studies which demonstrate the power of placebos. Here are some examples: Fisher et al. studied the efficacy of a drug in a controlled experiment designed to highlight the significance of the doctor's 'confidence' in the treatment. They trained some doctors to play a 'treatment-orientated role' and others a 'research-orientated role'. The former involved communicating to patients great confidence, while the latter physicians communicated grave doubts about its efficacy. The 'treatment-orientated' doctors were considerably more successful than their colleagues (Fisher, Cole, Rickels and Uhlenhuth, 1964).

The role of the experimenter's/prescriber's expectations *per se* is highlighted by the need to use double-blind methods. This is illustrated in Beecher's research into the efficacy of morphine. Investigations prior to this had obtained data differentiating morphine's effect from that of placebos. However, in these the doctors had always known when morphine as opposed to placebo was being administered. This, it seems, allowed the doctors' prophecy to become self-fulfilling because when Beecher made sure that neither the patient nor the doctor knew which of the two substances was being given, morphine was found to be no better than the placebo (Beecher, 1966).

The doctors' expectations are now generally recognised as being such a powerful influence in placebogenesis that no drug trial would be considered properly carried out unless double-blind techniques are used.

As we have seen the interest and behaviour of the therapist toward the patient is crucial. So also are the attitudes of other staff. Shapiro points out that their attitudes, expectations, biases, conflicts, and harmony can influence the power of placebos. He quotes a study which demonstrates that the effect of a placebo can be reduced from 70 per cent to 25 per cent if the negative attitude of the nurses toward a placebo injection is apparent to the patient. In another study, patients treated with placebos improved more than those on tranquilisers, a result the authors attributed to the bias of the nurses against chemotherapy (Volgyesi, and Baker and Thorpe, quoted in Shapiro, 1971).

One of the more dramatic instances of a placebo in psychiatric medicine is that of Sakel's insulin coma treatment of schizophrenia. The use of insulin increased from 1949 to become a very widespread form of treatment. It involved inducing a coma in psychotic patients and was undoubtedly dangerous but 'good' results of this treatment were found. By 1963 it had been found to be no more, and no less we might add, than a very powerful form of placebo, and dropped almost completely from the treatment repertoire (Rachman, 1971). Shapiro points out that the interest and attention of the staff, necessitated by the dangers during treatment, may have accounted for its success. Patients were selectively chosen and were, in effect, a therapeutic elite. The facts that the treatment was expensive, fashionable, elaborate, detailed, time consuming and esoteric, all combined to heighten the attention that the patients got during and after treatment (Shapiro, 1971).

This example is of particular interest because although the effects of behaviour on placebo power are clearly demonstrated, the relationship between this behaviour and its proceeding expectations are complex. On the one hand it is safe to assume that in its heyday there was a powerful prophecy that insulin coma treatment would work. But there is another prophecy at work, the anti-self-fulfilling prophecy mentioned in the second chapter. The danger probably heightened the power of this placebo because it caused the doctors and staff to expect that this patient could die. It was necessary to avoid this prophecy being fulfilled and so it precipitated higher levels of 'curative' behaviour, thus defeating it.

This is an important example because of this demonstration of the complex way in which self-fulfilling prophecies sometimes work. Also it makes clear that the crucial factor is what the prophets *do* and not just what they believe. But an amazing fact has largely been overlooked in the story of the rise and fall of insulin coma treatment. For years it worked!! Further research did not disprove the results, it revealed that it was not the insulin coma, but the *other factors* which produced the improvement. But the medical profession gave up the treatment lock, stock and barrel.

This is why it is argued here that we must turn these so-called 'artifacts' on their heads and understand their workings in order to maximise their effect. Or put another way we should try to do all that was done in insulin coma therapy, but save money on the insulin because that is the only link in the chain which has been proved faulty.

The last and perhaps most surprising example demonstrates the power of the doctors' enthusiastic 'selling' of a placebo. Park and Covi took a group of psychoneurotic adult patients and gave them placebos telling them exactly what they were! Their actual words were 'Many people with your kind of condition have also been helped by what are sometimes called sugar pills, and we feel that a so-called sugar pill may help you too. Do you know what a sugar pill is? A sugar pill is a pill with no medicine in it at all. I think this pill will help you as it has helped so many others. Are you willing to try this pill?' One patient, laughed at by her husband for taking an inactive pill, did not take the pills, the others did—and their conditions improved! The writers conclude that the enthusiastic way the pills were sold to the patients must have been a crucial variable in their success (Park and Covi, 1965).

The placebo examples above clearly indicate the importance of the three stages of the self-fulfilling prophecy. Park and Covi, Fisher *et al.* and Beecher emphasise the role of prophecy while the insulin coma example and the review by Shapiro demonstrate the second stage; the prophecy-based behaviour of the treatment staff. Given these two stages then placebos have been shown to be effective in a wide range of conditions, thus confirming the positive expectations of doctors and patients. Misdirected though these expectations may be at the start, they can nevertheless prove correct.

Conclusions

It can then be concluded that experimenter bias, the hypnotist's influence and the placebo effect all demonstrate that expectations can work as self-fulfilling prophecies in the interaction between the professional, that is experimenter, hypnotist, doctor or nurse and the client, be he 'subject' or patient.

We should also bear in mind that the effects of this mechanism are not only in one direction. Rosenthal has demonstrated that expectations and biases in any direction can influence outcome (Rosenthal, 1966, 1969; Rosenthal and Jacobson, 1968). Barber does not relate his findings to any specific response but to a variety of behaviours (Barber, 1969). Shapiro has indicated that the placebo effect can be both curative and harmful as in the production of side effects and the counteracting of 'potent active drugs' (Shapiro, 1971).

What then is the relevance of these findings for the study of the helping relationship? The following observation by Rosenthal and Frank points the way:

> The similarity of the forces operating in psychotherapy and the placebo effect may account for the high consistency of improvement rates found with various therapies, from that conducted by physicians without psychiatric training to intensive psychoanalysis. This explanation gains plausibility from the fact that reported improvement rates for various series of neurotics treated by different forms of psychotherapy hover around 60 per cent. This is the same as that reported for the placebo effect in illnesses in which emotional components may play a major role such as 'colds' and headaches (Rosenthal and Frank, 1956, p. 297).

The similarity is further reinforced when we consider Rosenthal's finding that approximately 60 per cent of subjects gave responses consistent with the expectation of their experimenter (Rosenthal, 1969).

We will discuss the process of the interaction in which these expectations are communicated and acted upon, and the characteristics of the potent prophet and responsive client in later chapters. Let us now move on to look at the evidence from psychotherapy research that self-fulfilling prophecy mechanisms operate.

Chapter four

Prophecy in helping relationships

The three main areas of evidence presented here are the placebogenesis of therapy, the role of hope and faith and the direct research evidence that expectations influence therapy. It might be timely to remind readers of the framework outlined in the first chapter, that is that we are interested in all worker-client interactions designed to bring about change. We should perhaps also underline that 'therapy' does not necessarily imply the acceptance or use of a medical model.

Is psychotherapy a placebo?

Rosenthal and Frank have shown, theoretically, how the process of 'psychotherapy' has distinct similarities to the placebo effect (Rosenthal and Frank, 1956). It has been argued in the preceding chapter that the placebo effect and other forms of interpersonal interaction are similar phenomena. Thus, if expectations work as a self-fulfilling prophecy in the placebo effect it could be an important variable in the 'psychotherapy' process too.

The relationship between placebos and 'psychotherapy' is supported by several research studies. In the first of these psychiatric outpatients were first given six months' group, individual or minimal psychotherapy. It was found that, while the degree of improvement in social effectiveness was related to the amount of treatment contact, average diminution of discomfort was the same for all forms of therapy. It was suggested that the results indicated that relief of discomfort was due mainly to the 'mobilization of the patient's trust'. This view was later tested by the administration of a chemical placebo to twelve of the original sample two or three years *after* the original project. These were all patients who had shown improvement but had subsequently regressed. The placebo produced similar results to the original therapy sessions. This led the experimenters to conclude that it was the therapist's ability to 'mobilize the patient's expectation of help' that was the crucial variable (Gliedman, Nash, Imber, Stone and Frank, 1958; Frank, Gliedman, Imber, Nash and Stone, 1959).

The second study illustrates the potency of expectancy in behaviour therapy techniques. In this research a process of desensitisation of animal phobias in college students was compared with a process named 'T-scope therapy'. This latter test was in fact a bogus process but was presented as a highly effective one complete with falsified records of test results. It proved to be highly effective, in fact as effective as systematic desensitisation. To check these results another group were given 'T-scope therapy' but told that a crucial element would be omitted so that no improvement could be expected. Both this sample and a control, no treatment group did not show a reduction in phobic behaviour. The communication of high expectations would then seem to account for the success of 'T-scope therapy' (Marcia, Rubin and Efran, 1969).

McReynolds added further evidence to these findings and found that the more sophisticated the placebo and genuine its presentation the greater the degree of improvement in his subjects (McReynolds, Barnes, Brooks and Remagen, 1973).

In these examples we see that the administration of a placebo procedure proved to be as successful as a variety of therapeutic procedures. The latter experiments also clearly indicate that the *behaviour* of the therapist/experimenter, that is the deliberate arousal of hope and high expectations of success and his genuineness, are not only crucial variables but those which produce change. Therefore these examples demonstrate that expectations can work in therapy towards a self-fulfilling prophecy.

The role of hope

Religions have stressed the crucial necessity of faith if man is to change and control his destiny. The social sciences have followed more cautiously. Freud and Jung both referred to the importance of the hope and faith of the patient in life generally and the treatment process in particular (Freud, 1963; Jung, 1933). Halmos has outlined the importance of faith and hope in counselling procedures (a generic term covering the activity of the helping professions engaged in 'talking cures') (Halmos, 1965). Existentialist writers have outlined how therapy can be a search for faith and hope, for order in the world and how adjustment to these questions may be an essential characteristic of the therapist (Colm, 1966). One is reminded of Erikson's view that we cannot expect children to come to terms with 'life' if their parents cannot accept 'death' (Erikson, 1965).

Karl Menninger (1964) summed up the dangers of lack of hope when he pointed out that mental illness was incurable because psychiatrists and others had lost faith and hope. He was writing of an earlier time and went on to say that now the mentally ill were regarded as 'curable' and so proved to be. But perhaps he is being over-optimistic. When one considers the prognosis often attached to clients diagnosed as 'schizophrenic', or as suffering from any psychotic condition, or described as a 'recidivist', it is doubtful whether much hope is held that they will show positive change. The common culture has a saying about leopards never changing their spots.

We might digress a little to illustrate the significance of this stage of the argument by re-introducing the labelling theory position. Remember that the previous outline of the theory emphasised that implied in the labelling process was a prediction about the future, and that essentially the prediction was that the deviant would continue to be deviant—once a thief always a thief. There is a growing literature which discusses the implications of these processes and the harm they can do (Goffman, 1968; Cooper, 1970; Laing, 1969a, 1969b; Becker, 1973; Scheff, 1975).

Jerome Frank was one of the first to discuss thoroughly the role of hope in helping relationships. He reviews the literature on 'healing processes' generally from the pre-scientific rituals of witch doctors through placebo medicine to modern forms of psychoanalysis. He also looks at processes of change from religious revivalism to communist thought reform. His focus for doing so is to deduce the important characteristics and variables which are common to them all (Frank, 1973). A positive ingredient of all healing processes which he identified is that of the *hope* of the patient and therapist. He does this by systematically developing the observation that man is unique, in as much as he includes the future in his consciousness and experience (Frank, 1968, 1973; see also Jung, 1933; Kelly, 1955; Rychlak, 1968; Bannister and Fransella, 1971). Implicit in this view is the belief that man is not completely predetermined by his past experiences, no matter how damaging they may have been, and that change is possible. The more recent findings of 'maternal deprivation' research provides support for this view (Clarke, 1968; Brown, 1968; Grygier, Chesley and Tuters, 1969).

Frank links his views of hope in therapy to the workings of placebos, focusing on the findings that both have effect in reducing anxiety and guilt. He explains that the relief of anxiety and depression frees the patient to make better use of the healthy parts of his personality so that he functions more effectively in general (Frank, 1968, 1973; Shapiro, 1971; Calestro, 1972). Frank shows us that the therapist's ability to overcome the patient's mistrust, founded on his history of pathology, is a prerequisite of a constructive healing process. The therapist must offer the patient a contrasting, positive experience, part of which is the raising of the clients positive expectations, i.e. arousing hope. He also sees hope as a catalyst or essential antecedent to constructive personality change. This, he argues, is because hope is a fundamental ingredient of expectations of the future and these expectations may well determine the behaviour of the individual. Thus 'the mobilization of the patients' positive expectations' is a crucial task (Frank, 1968).

We have already noted that experimenter bias and placebos can work for both better or for worse—and so it is with hope. Frank warns us that the lack of hope 'can delay recovery or even hasten death'. This is supported by evidence that 'giving up' and a deterioration of interest and hope for the future can accelerate the course of certain physical illnesses such as certain forms of cancer. Again we are reminded of the powers attributed to labelling (Schmale and Iker, 1965; Schmale, 1969). Seligman, in attempting to define a new theory of depression, illustrates many striking examples of how animals and people can learn to be helpless which involves giving up hope. He discusses a growing body of research which demonstrates that this process can result in stunted development, depression and even death (Seligman, 1975).

We should note that Frank's view is consistent with that outlined in chapter 1, that therapy is based on the interaction between therapist and patient, change is seen as a result of this interaction and indeed he has shown the extent to which patients can be influenced in what they say and do by the therapist (Frank, 1973). Basically he argues that patient's liking, trust, and confidence in his therapist are the foundations for patient hope (Frank, 1968). There is a growing body of empirical findings supporting the view that the beliefs of the client seem crucial. Kelly states that the change that occurs in therapy will be directly related to the expectations the client brings to the situation (Kelly, 1955). We should also note that the client's belief in himself as a source of hope (Cartwright and Cartwright, 1958) and his positive attitudes towards counselling (Lipkin, 1954) will all influence outcome. In short, the patient's prognostic expectations are of crucial significance and affect outcome for better or for worse (Goldstein, 1962). We should note, however, that in these studies the therapist's expectations are held to be constant. We will see later that it is the interaction between client's and therapist's expectations that is crucial and that we cannot consider one without the other.

These findings, the work of Frank and many of the placebo studies, concentrate on the hope and expectations of the patient. However, the central focus here is on the potency of the *expectations of the therapist or professional change agent.* It is important to consider the expectations of the client inasmuch as they also affect the 'interaction', but more will be said of this in the next chapter. At this stage let us move on to the expectations of the therapist and the evidence to show that these can act as a self-fulfilling prophecy or as Goldstein calls them 'prognostic expectations'.

Expectations and behaviour in helping relationships

There is evidence to support the hypothesis that the professional helper's expectations and attitudes toward treatment influence the outcome of the relationship in the direction of those expectations. Drayer found that disaster victims were highly susceptible to the influence of the behaviour expected of them by their helpers (Drayer, 1956). Goldstein and Shipman studied symptom reduction of patients after their initial psychiatric interviews. They found this to be significantly related to the favourable or unfavourable attitudes the psychotherapists (senior medical students) had towards the type of treatment they were attempting (Goldstein and Shipman, 1961).

Goldstein studied the effects of prognostic expectations in a research programme designed to analyse the effect of both patient and therapist attitudes. He took two 'treatment' groups (a) therapy, experimental group and (b) no-therapy, control group; totalling thirty patients to be treated by ten therapists. The experimental group was then divided into those who perceived their problems as improving over the course of fifteen sessions and those who felt their problems got worse. Then the therapists of these two groups were compared in terms of their initial prognostic expectations. The therapists of the patients who perceived positive change in themselves during therapy, expected significantly more patient improvement than did the therapists for those patients who perceived negative change in themselves (Goldstein, 1960). These findings confirmed the similar relationship between expectation and outcome found by Erika Chance (Chance, 1959).

However, these writers tend to focus on the belief rather than the reciprocal behaviour involved. Frank, for example, puts forward the argument that the predominant factor is that the therapist communicates his belief to the patient and that the patient believes because of the former's credibility and the latter's suggestibility. He speculates that the prophecy is communicated by a variety of ways, perhaps even by telepathy (Frank, 1973).

It will be shown as we develop the model in this and the next chapter that our focus is the *behaviour* of therapist and client. This is a change of emphasis and does not deny the importance of beliefs, indeed it is upon these that the behaviour is based. But it is hoped that by changing the emphasis and applying the self-fulfilling prophecy model we can carry our understanding further.

Having established that there probably is a link between expectations and outcome let us turn our attention to the model and ask: do therapists with positive expectations behave differently toward their clients from those who have negative attitudes?

Fiedler notes that in order to have a patient who expresses his feelings freely one must be a therapist who has favourable attitudes toward his patient (Fiedler, 1953). Truax and Carkhuff note in a review of research literature that the prognosis and the therapist's expectations can help influence the level of 'therapeutic conditions' that he is willing to offer

(Truax and Carkhuff, 1964). Strupp provides us with empirical evidence to support this link between expectations and behaviour: a sound film of an initial interview between a neurotic patient and a relatively inexperienced therapist was made. The film was cut and twenty-eight pauses of thirty seconds were introduced. The film was then shown to fifty-five psychiatrists and fifty-five psychologists who were asked to assume the role of therapist. They were asked what they would have said during each thirty second pause. Following the film they then completed a comprehensive questionnaire outlining their diagnostic and prognostic impressions, their treatment plans and attitudes towards the patient.

The results indicated the extent of favourable prognosis correlated with the favourable attitudes of the therapist towards the client. Those stating negative prognostic expectations were more likely to anticipate acting out by the patient. The psychologist's prognostic estimates correlated significantly and positively with their ratings of the degree of patient insight, ego-strength, and self-observation versus rationalisation; and negatively with the degree of patient disturbance.

Those therapists providing a non-committed prognostic estimate tended to show more 'warm' responses and great initiative in their communications than did both the favourable and unfavourable sample. They also gave the smallest number of silent responses. Therapists whose prognosis was unfavourable gave more than four times as many 'cold' responses than did favourable prognosticators (Strupp, 1960). These findings were supported by two further investigations in this research programme (Strupp and Williams, 1960; Wallach and Strupp, 1960). Sheasby, in a content analysis of Probation Officers' files, also found that workers who had positive expectations of their clients behaved in a more confident, positive and skilful way towards them than they did with clients for whom they had not recommended to the court that supervision would be helpful (Sheasby, 1971). Frank reviews evidence that shows how the frequency and length of treatment sessions is dependent upon the therapist's expectations (Frank, 1973).

Rosenhan in his fascinating study 'On Being Sane in Insane Places', revealed that his subjects, who were sane but manipulated their diagnostic interview so that they were diagnosed psychotic, were treated very differently by all the staff from 'normal' people. Communication was very poor and often bizarre; for example one subject asked a doctor 'Pardon me Dr X, could you tell me when I am eligible for ground privileges?' to be answered, 'Good morning, Dave. How are you today?' The doctor then moved on without waiting for the reply. The patients were thus treated impersonally and made to feel powerless. Much of their behaviour was interpreted as being 'part of their madness'. The underlying prediction about their future was underlined when they were discharged. None of them was described as being 'cured' or free from their 'illness', but ascertained as still suffering from schizophrenia but in 'remission'. (There was one exception, he was diagnosed 'manic depressive'.) These subjects were not only generally 'sane' but from the moment of their admission into hospital had exhibited no symptoms of illness at all (Rosenhan, 1973).

The power of expectations in the diagnosis and thus treatment of psychiatric conditions was also demonstrated by Temerlin. He presented a group of psychiatrists, clinical psychologists and graduate students in clinical psychology with a normal healthy man (as adjudged by three clinical psychologists and the control group in the experiment), who was in fact an actor following a script designed to emphasise his health. The experimental group were then told that a highly prestigious member of their profession had said that he was interesting because although he looks neurotic he was in fact psychotic. The results clearly illustrate that the subjects' diagnosis was heavily biased by this expectation.

The implications, discussed in detail later, would seem to be crucial to many workers in the helping professions who receive their referrals from someone else who has already decided that the person 'needs help' (Temerlin, 1968).

It seems fairly clear, then, that the types of expectations or prophecy the therapist makes are inseparable from his behaviour towards his client. It is also true that these factors are inseparable from the therapist's feelings of liking and general attitudes towards the client, thereby confirming our view that the 'total person' of the therapist, and not just his intellectual knowledge, is important.

The second question we need to ask is: does this behaviour lead to the outcome in the direction of the expectations? A brief summary shows us that negative expectations and poor prognosis lead the therapist to be cold toward his clients, spend less time with them, be more impersonal, like them less, discourage them to reveal their feelings and generally credit them with less personality resources and allow them less power. In short the therapist with negative or poor expectations seems to have taken Jay Haley's advice on the 'Art of being a Failure as a Therapist', and is sticking to the motto named by Haley as 'the five B's which Guarantee Dynamic Failure: Be Passive, Be Inactive, Be Reflective, Be Silent, Beware' (Haley, 1969).

By contrast the therapists who had positive expectations or were non-committal showed more warmth and greater initiative (which we interpret as more strenuous attempts to understand), they liked their clients more and attributed more positive personality resources to the client. One is strongly reminded of Rosenthal's remarks about the attitudes of his experimenters to the 'bright' rats, and Shapiro's summary of the importance of the attitudes and expectations of staff, reviewed in the last chapter.

The growing body of research evidence on the factors which promote positive change as a result of therapy confirms these behaviour factors as fulfilling the prophecy of the therapist. These behaviour attributes fit into the scheme of accurate empathy, non-possessive warmth and genuineness, which have been underlined as crucial to positive therapeutic outcome (Rogers, 1954, 1957, 1961, 1966; Truax and Carkhuff, 1967; Carkhuff, 1969; Truax and Mitchell, 1971; Goldstein, 1975; Egan, 1975).

Further evidence that self-fulfilling prophecies are at work in psychotherapeutic relationships is implied in more recent work done on the significance of social class and psychotherapy. Goldstein summarises the arguments in his book *Structured Learning Therapy: Toward a Psychotherapy for the Poor.* He points out that contemporary psychotherapy is predominantly carried out by middle-class therapists for middle-class patients. The self-fulfilling prophecy model can be shown to be significant in the analysis of the relevant research. Goldstein reports work which indicates that lower-class patients are far more likely to be considered psychotic, alcoholic and generally to be ascertained as having poorer mental health and a poorer prognosis. He also summarises evidence which indicates that lower-class patients are less likely to elicit the same degree of attention, empathy, warmth and willingness to treat from therapists as middle-class patients. Lower-class patients are also shown to be far less likely to be taken off the waiting list, far more likely to terminate outpatient treatment and more likely to be hospitalised as psychotic (Goldstein, 1973).

The link between the poor outcome of psychotherapy with lower-class patients and the behaviour of therapists is clear. Although the causal link between the negative prognosis and that behaviour is not explicit it is difficult to believe that the one is not a direct result of the other. The view is supported by Lerner and Fiske's study outlined below.

Incidentally Goldstein explains the poor outcome of treatment partly in terms of the clash of expectations between patient and therapist. That is, whereas the therapist meets the lower-class client with low expectations characteristically these patient's expectations are very high. We will say more about effective levels of expectations and the potency of prophets in chapter 7 but at this stage we should note that it is the therapist's prophecy and not the patient's which is fulfilled.

Confirmation of this view is to be found in the research of Lerner and Fiske. This study deals with the client attributes, which had previously been related to outcome, of thirty clients treated by fourteen therapists. The study failed to replicate previous findings that these attributes, which were related to social class and severity of impairment, were related to outcome. However, the findings of these investigators led them to suggest that outcome is affected by the attributes and beliefs of therapists concerning the prognosis for lower-class and severely disturbed clients. Those workers who specialised in, and thought they were reasonably good at, working with the underprivileged clients *were* able to help (Lerner and Fiske, 1973).

Conclusions

We can, then, now conclude that expectations influence the outcome of therapy relationships in the direction of the expectation. By looking at available research evidence we can see that expectations influence behaviour and that the behaviour precipitated is compatible with the outcome predicted. In short, the self-fulfilling prophecy model outlined in the second chapter can be used to demonstrate the power of expectations in relationships which bring about change. It has also been shown that self-fulfilling prophecies can work in any direction, and that self-fulfilling prophecies can operate when expectations are overt or implicit and when the communication of the prophecy is explicit, general or by a very personal, subtle process. Specification of the details of these mechanisms and the characteristics of the personalities of client and worker that maximise these conditions are discussed later.

Having established the validity of our central hypothesis we may now ask the question: how do self-fulfilling prophecies work?

Chapter five

Behaviour and change

When we look at the details of the interaction between professional helpers and their clients we move into the realm of speculation. Little hard information is available, the bulk of research having been done on either therapist characteristics (see Truax and Mitchell, 1971), or client variables (see Garfield, 1971). But little is focused on what actually happens between them in the interview situation. The work of Rogers and his followers are notable exceptions (Rogers and Dymond, 1954; Rogers, 1961, 1967; Truax and Carkhuff, 1967; Carkhuff, 1969). The growing use of video taping with its opportunity to scrutinise what really happens will perhaps improve our knowledge. We should also note that analysis of process needs to be linked to analysis of outcome if it is to serve any significant purpose in increasing our knowledge of how to help the client (Truax and Mitchell, 1971).

However, having thus outlined some of the difficulties facing us in this area let us tentatively attempt to analyse how the prophecies/expectations of the therapist are communicated to the client and how they influence his behaviour.

The communication of expectations

The reader will remember that when we discussed Rosenthal's work we pointed out that his control group design enabled him to consider the communication of expectations/biases or prophecies as a separate topic. In outlining the evidence *vis-à-vis* this communication we can highlight its similarities to the 'behaviour' aspects outlined as the middle stage of self-fulfilling prophecies identified in experimenter influence, placebo effects and 'psychotherapy' research.

Verbal communication seems to be a key feature in transmitting expectations. Rosenthal, in his summary of relevant research, shows us that experimenter bias can be communicated by tape-recorded instructions, thus controlling for non-auditory signals (Rosenthal, 1969). The work by Barber confirms this. He found that hypnotic suggestions were equally dependent upon verbal communications and indeed that tape recordings were often as effective as the presence of an experimenter (Barber, 1969). Truax and Carkhuff illustrate how the effective ingredients of a therapist's behaviour can be illustrated from sound tape recordings thus supporting this view (Truax and Carkhuff, 1967). However, non-verbal channels of communication are not without significance (remember Clever Hans in chapter 2) and Rosenthal concludes that there is evidence that both visual and auditory clues are of importance in communicating bias, but especially the latter.

We should point out here that we do not have to assume that the expectation or prophecy is overtly communicated. If we look back to our insulin coma treatment example we can see that in these circumstances it is the 'behaviour', i.e. greater attention etc., of the medical staff which brought about improvement. This 'attention etc.' was precipitated not only by the prophecy—'insulin coma treatment works', but also by a subsidiary expectation—'the treatment is highly dangerous and patients can easily die during it'.

Rosenthal also noticed in his experiments that his experimenters found their subjects more 'likeable and behaved in a more pleasant, friendly and enthusiastic way towards them'. These characteristics we saw in chapter 3 were features of those therapists who had positive expectations of their clients and who were thus more likely to have successful

53

outcomes to their treatment. Shapiro also reports that interest, warmth, friendliness and liking for the patient are important in positive placebo response (Shapiro, 1971). (We will see more similarities such as these emerging when we consider the characteristics of the potent prophet and the responsive client in subsequent chapters.)

Further research into the Pygmalion effect more clearly illustrates how the effect works. Several studies demonstrate that it was the quality, rather than the quantity, of teacher-pupil interactions which changed after the expectation had been manipulated, thus positive communications increased, negative ones decreased, the subjects were praised more, more often smiled at and more often called upon to give answers (Kogan and Wimberger, 1971; Rubovits and Maehr, 1971; Meichenbaum, Bowers and Ross, 1969; Chaikin, Sigler and Derlega, 1974).

Reinforcement and prophecy fulfilment

Allport suggested in his example of the self-fulfilling prophecy that 'expectations seek out their own reinforcement' and that once the chain of expectations leading to behaviour, which reinforces that expectation, is set in motion it continues in a system of reinforcing feedback loops (Allport, 1950). This view of how expectations influence behaviour and find their own reinforcement is supported in other works (Kelly, 1955; Abercrombie, 1969), and more specifically has growing support in the field of professional helping relationships (Platonov, 1959; Goldstein, 1962; Krasner, 1962; Berenson and Carkhuff, 1967; Truax and Carkhuff, 1967; Carkhuff, 1969; Murray and Jacobson, 1971; Krasner and Ullman, 1973; Frank, 1973; Egan, 1975).

The first step in this argument is that the helping relationship is indeed, to some extent, a situation where the helper (therapist) influences the views, attitudes, assumptions and expectations of the client. There is mounting evidence that it is impossible for a therapist to intervene and not influence his client no matter how 'non-directive' he may attempt to be. Goldstein points out that Freud was aware of this danger and designed his interviewing methods accordingly (Goldstein, 1962; Krasner, 1962; Strupp, 1970, 1973; Egan, 1975; Frank, 1973). We know for instance that there is a tendency for patients to produce the dreams that will fit into their psychoanalysts' schema (Wolff, 1954) and that the client's moral values tend to shift in the direction of their therapist's (Rosenthal, 1955). There is also evidence that we teach clients a language for analysing the world. Heine, for example, found that patients treated by therapists of different 'schools' of therapy (psychoanalytic, non-directive and Adlerian) explained their 'improvement' in terms of the methods and in the language of those schools (Heine, 1953).

Murray tested the possibility of *not* communicating attitudes and beliefs to the patient by applying a content analysis to a verbatim 'non-directive' case published by Carl Rogers and found that one group of statements (primarily those indicating 'independence') were approved—or positively reinforced, while others were disapproved (including 'dependence', 'sexual material' and 'defenses') (Murray, 1956, see Murray and Jacobson, 1971). These findings have been replicated by Truax (Truax, 1966, see Truax and Carkhuff, 1967). However, the process need not be as subtle as these outlined above. Scheff has described how doctor and patient (or any two actors) may negotiate where the responsibility for behaviour—and thus the focus of treatment—lies (Scheff, 1968). Frank shows the similarities between these processes and more overt methods at the other end of the continuum such as brain-washing (Frank, 1973).

Having accepted that the helping relationship is indeed one where the therapist influences the client we can see how a conditioning model of reinforcement may explain the communication of expectations. Truax, Carkhuff and Berenson have recognised the importance of this type of model and outlined how the 'three characteristics of helping persons' serve as positive reinforcers (considered in more detail in the next chapter) (Truax and Carkhuff, 1967; Berenson and Carkhuff, 1967; Truax and Mitchell, 1971). We may illustrate this general position, including the role of hope in anxiety reduction, outlined in the previous chapter, with the following passage from Murray and Jacobson:

> In summary, the traditional therapeutic process now looks something like this: an anxious, conflicted patient enters therapy. The establishment of a dependent relationship provides an initial reduction in anxiety and an increase in hope and self-confidence. The therapist attempts to clarify, evaluate, and modify the patient's belief systems and to co-ordinate these cognitive changes with modifications in the patient's emotional and behavioural response system. The primary method he has for doing this is the systematic use of his own personality—his warmth, interest, sensitivity, and the like. It is probably these spontaneous and genuine verbal and emotional communications of the therapist that provide the basic social reinforcement and social influence in therapy. The therapist's verbal responses serve also as discriminative cues that convey information about the kinds of responses the patient can perform in order to maintain or elicit the emotional warmth and positive feelings of the therapist. Thus, the therapist uses an emotional lever in order to elicit anxiety-laden responses so that extinction, changes in belief systems, and emotional and behavioural changes can occur. Some of the most important of these changes occur within the context of the therapeutic relationship itself (Murray and Jacobson, 1971, p. 723).

Before describing the reinforcement spiral in operation *vis-à-vis* the therapist's expectations we should bear in mind that we have said that primarily it is an interactional process. That is to say it is the *client's* expectations and the therapist's prognostic expectations that are important (see chapter 4). In fact we see the model as focusing on the interaction of these sets of variables—i.e. the therapist's and the client's expectations.

We suggest then that expectations may influence the relationship in this way. The therapist (T), expects to be able to help the client. He, T, communicates this expectation to the client (C). C responds with relief from anxiety and communicates a degree of aroused hope. This is partly because he has found potential relief from his problems and partly because his expectation that his problems are soluble has been reinforced. T reads the relief from anxiety and emerging hope and his expectation that he will be able to help is reinforced. T's expectations thus strengthened are communicated with more certainty which provides stronger reinforcement for C who in turn . . . and so on.

The same type of model would apply to expected behaviour change. T would expect C to behave in a particular way, for example more independently. C shows some signs of doing so, these will be perceived and reinforced by T. C then seeks further reinforcement from T by providing more indications of independence which reinforce T's expectations and strengthen them, thus T provides greater reinforcement for C . . . and so on. We can see how this spiral of reinforcement behaviour is the middle behaviour-stage of the self-fulfilling prophecy, precipitated by the original expectations and causing the prophesied behaviour.

The writer believes that the evidence presented so far supports this type of model while recognising the necessity to test it in practice. Perhaps when we have more precise tools for analysing the moment-by-moment interaction of interviews it will be possible to do research to test this hypothesis. At present, it is hoped that the next chapter on the client-centred therapy as a self-fulfilling prophecy will lend weight to this analysis.

Modelling and prophecy fulfilment

Before leaving this section we must point out that the potency of expectations may be explained in terms of modelling. Rosenthal comments on the importance of these concepts in communication of experimenter bias (Rosenthal, 1969). Truax and Carkhuff demonstrated the value of 'pre-treatment training' by playing a tape recording of a 'good' therapy session to prospective patients who then tended to model themselves on this interaction pattern (Truax and Carkhuff, 1967). We suggest that a therapist displaying an optimistic view of the patient's problems may serve as a helpful model, just as one who, when faced with the client's problems thinks the situation is hopeless, will cause the client further distress. The awareness of modelling procedures as part of a programme of planned change may well prove to be an important asset (Bandura, 1971; Krasner and Ullman, 1973).

Carkhuff stresses the importance of the helping person as a model by pointing out that if the helper cannot develop his own potentials, he cannot enable another to do so (Carkhuff, 1969). Rogers, and other client-centred writers, have stressed the need for the therapist to be 'congruent and genuine', i.e. mature individuals unafraid of their own feelings and weaknesses.

In short, unless we settle for a situation where the 'blind lead the blind' the professional helper has to work from a position of personal strength and security and prophecise that he can have success in coping with and finding a solution to the client's problems—any other prophecy he makes is just as likely to be fulfilled!

These conclusions have been deduced from a variety of research in related fields as well as those more directly relevant to helping relationships. I think sufficient cumulative evidence has been presented to justify accepting our central hypothesis. However, this does not deny that it is necessary to test it fully with direct research on the three stages of the prophecy and the causal links between them. This research will of necessity focus on the second behaviour stage of the self-fulfilling prophecy in order to test the suggested model of operating. It is also necessary that the 'helpful' and possibly 'harmful' aspects of this behaviour are further identified so as to inform professional helpers so that their practice can become more reliable.

Chapter six

Client-centred therapy: an example

So far we have talked about the self-fulfilling prophecy as the way in which expectations work in the interaction of the change process. We are now going to use this concept to analyse those characteristics of the helping person which have been shown to be essential. In doing so we hope to highlight the crucial fundamental role of expectations and thus underline their importance in the helping process. It is proposed that we do this by using quotations by client-centred writers to make explicit what is implicit and so illustrate each of the three stages of the self-fulfilling prophecy. Carl Rogers will provide the pivot for this discussion, with other writers, notably Truax and Carkhuff, providing corroborating evidence based on empirical research.

The prophecy

'Man is capable of consciously directing his own fate, as long as he has not become so bound up with neurotic defenses that he loses his freedom to act' (Rogers, 1961, p. 193).

We can see that Rogers makes a stand against determinism believing essentially in the potential for free choice in all men. This is, however, qualified by 'neurotic defenses' as well as the pressures of the external (to the individual) environment: 'the fully functioning person . . . not only experiences but utilizes the most absolute freedom when he spontaneously freely and voluntarily chooses and wills that which is also absolutely determined' (Rogers, 1961, p. 193).

But, we may ask, why should man strive to direct his own fate? Why should clients improve and change? Rogers's answers to these questions further reveal his optimistic outlook with the formulation of the 'Growth Hypothesis'. 'In most if not all individuals there exist growth forces, tendencies toward self-actualization, which may act as the sole motivation for therapy . . . the individual has the capacity and the strength to devise, quite unaided, the steps which will lead him to a more mature and more comfortable relationship to his reality' (Rogers, 1946, quoted in Rogers, 1966, p. 193).

Rogers answers criticism of this view, particularly the phrase 'quite unaided', by explaining that he still holds that basically no direct advice or aid need be given (Rogers, 1966). Here we must modify Rogers' emphasis on non-directiveness. We have shown in the last chapter how therapy is to some degree always a form of influence (a study referred to highlighting this was based on a Rogerian interview!) (Murray, 1956). However, we acknowledge that even so the potential for self-direction must be present if it is to be later reinforced, but this will become clearer as we proceed.

Rogers develops his positive view of the 'fully functioning person':

Contrary to those therapists who see depravity at man's core, who see men's deepest instincts as destructive, I have found that when man is truly free to become what he most deeply is, free to actualize his nature as an organism capable of awareness, then he clearly appears to move toward wholeness and integration. As I have put this elsewhere: When (man) is most fully man, when he is his complete organism, when awareness of experience, that peculiarly human attribute, is most fully operating, then he is to be trusted, then his behaviour is constructive. It is not always conventional.

61

It will not always be conforming. It will be individualized. But it will also be socialized (Rogers, 1966, p. 193).

'The theory proposes that the individual, after therapy will behave in ways which are less defensive, more socialized, more accepting of reality in himself and in his social environment, and will give more evidence of a socialized system of values' (Rogers and Dymond, 1954).

Rogers believes that therapy, when necessary, can help people 'bound up with neurotic defenses' to realise these potentials and bring about positive changes in their *'self-concept'*:

If I can create a relationship characterized on my part by a *genuineness* and transparency in which I am my real feelings; by a warm *acceptance* of and prizing of the other person as a separate individual; by a *sensitive ability to see his world* and himself as he sees them; then the other individual in the relationship: will experience and understand aspects of himself which previously he has repressed; will find himself becoming better integrated, more able to function effectively; will become more similar to the person he would like to be; will be more self-directing—and self-confident; will become more of a person, more unique and more self-expressive; will be more understanding, more accepting of others; will be able to cope with the problems of life more adequately and more comfortably (Rogers, 1961, p. 37).

We can see then what sort of expectations Rogers has of his clients and the hope and faith he has in their potential to achieve these goals. We will see that the characteristics of the 'helping person' are remarkably similar.

Rogers it seems is aware of the power of relationship in shaping behaviour and implicitly maybe the self-fulfilling prophecy—in criticising 'behaviour therapy':

If we see the relationship as an opportunity to reinforce

certain types of words or opinions in the other, then I tend to see him as an object—a basically mechanical, manipulable object. And if I see this as his potentiality, he tends to act in ways which support this hypothesis. If on the other hand I see a relationship as an opportunity to 'reinforce' all that he is, the person that he is with all his existent potentialities, then he tends to act in ways which support this hypothesis . . . . Personally I prefer this second type of hypothesis (Rogers, 1961, p. 56).

The paradox in the above quotation (i.e. rejecting behaviour therapy yet saying 'reinforcement' can alter what a man is) clearly outlines where Rogers departs from the pure behaviour therapists. That departure is not basically in how therapy works but in his basic optimistic picture of man as a *total* being, with the internal potential for change, growth and development into the rational freedom of 'maturity'. Let us now move on to the second stage.

The behaviour

It is not surprising that Rogers's view of the 'fully functioning person' should be personified in the helping person. He believes that we can only help from a position of strength, a position we argued in the last chapter. There is a growing mass of literature on the characteristics of the effective helping person (Rogers, 1957, 1961, 1966; Truax and Carkhuff, 1964, 1967; Berenson and Carkhuff, 1967; Carkhuff, 1969, 1971; Egan, 1975).

However, the writer feels that the essence has been pin-pointed in the following passage:

Three characteristics of an effective therapist emerge from the divergent viewpoints: (1) an effective therapist is non-phoney, non-defensive, and authentic or *GENUINE* in his therapeutic encounter [Rogers used the term *congruent*]; (2) an effective therapist is able to provide a non-threatening, safe, trusting, or secure atmosphere through his own acceptance, positive regard, love, valuing, or *NON-POSSESSIVE WARMTH* for the client [Rogers called this *'Unconditional positive regard'*]; and (3) an effective therapist is able to understand, 'be with', 'grasp the meaning of', or have a high degree of *ACCURATE EMPATHIC UNDERSTANDING* of the client on a moment-by-moment basis (Truax and Mitchell, 1971, p. 302, my insertions).

These characteristics are active not passive, they refer to *behaviour not ideas* and *they must be explicitly communicated through the interaction to the client* and consciously perceived by him!!

Now we may ask, do these characteristics arise out of the beliefs and expectations put forward above as the prophecy? The writer thinks they do. We may note generally that 'accepting' a client for treatment implies a degree of self-worth to the client and also reinforces any expectation that he may have that he can change (Murray and Jacobson, 1971). But the client-centred approach is more than that. It is difficult to imagine that a therapist can be 'genuine', 'transparent', 'non-phoney', 'non-defensive', 'warm', 'accepting', 'loving', 'valuing' toward a client if he sees 'depravity at man's core' and man's 'deepest instincts as destructive'. Nor would we expect a therapist to be motivated to have a 'sensitive ability to see the client's world' and 'be with' the client on a 'moment-by-moment basis' if he did not believe he was seeking positive potential that is *'there'*.

Truax and Carkhuff have implicitly underlined this relationship:

Thus most therapists, and indeed other hospital and clinical personnel because of their prejudices, are usually unable or unwilling to provide high levels of therapeutic conditions to less desirable patients and therefore such patients show less constructive change. The suggestion is that therapist and others show, for example, less warmth and accurate empathic understanding to the patient who is less likeable to the therapist because of his age, his religious preference, or even his type of emotional disturbance; how many psychopathic deviates, for example receive high levels of warmth and accurate empathy from therapists? (Truax and Carkhuff, 1964).

(We have seen in chapter 4 the relationship between positive prognosis and the therapist 'liking' his client and will refer to it again in chapter 7.)

We have argued both in this and the previous chapter that accurate empathy, non-possessive warmth and genuineness can act as reinforcers. Let us finish our discussion of the behaviour stage of the client-centred self-fulfilling prophecy with the following explanation of how these characteristics reinforce generally, and specifically, aspects of Rogers' prophecy:

> It is tentatively theorized that accurate empathy, non-possessive warmth, genuineness and other therapeutic interpersonal skills have indirect effects upon patient change in four modalities: (1) they serve to reinforce positive aspects of the patient self-concept, modifying the existing self-concepts and thereby leading to changes in the patient's own self-reinforcement system; (2) they serve to reinforce self-exploratory behaviour and thereby elicit self-concepts and anxiety-laden material that can be then modified by selective reinforcement; (3) they serve to extinguish anxiety or fear responses associated with specific cues, both those elicited by the relationship with the therapist and those elicited by patient self-exploration; and (4) they serve to reinforce human relating, encountering, or interacting, and serve to extinguish fear or avoidance responses associated with human relating (Truax and Mitchell, 1971, p. 322).

Thus we can see the relationship between 'prophecy' and how it works in practice in the 'behaviour' stage of the interaction between therapist and client. We may add to

65

this description of the interactional/reinforcement model by our references to the prophecy working on a modelling principle. We can see, as we have already noted in Rogers' examples, the similarity between how the therapist should behave—and the basic prophecy for what the client may/will become like after treatment. Rogers in fact is quite specific in seeing the therapist's and the client's goal as identical, i.e. to become a 'fully functioning person' (Rogers, 1961). Carkhuff has also highlighted these factors, claiming that the characteristics of the 'helping person' are ones that should be adopted by all and not confined to a professional setting (Carkhuff, 1969).

The outcome

We do not propose to dwell on the detail of outcome studies here. We have mentioned elsewhere the growing body of research evidence supporting the view that accurate empathy, non-possessive warmth and genuineness lead to improved client functioning (Rogers and Dymond, 1954; Rogers, 1957, 1961, 1966; Truax, 1963; Truax and Carkhuff, 1964, 1967; Carkhuff, 1969).

In a review of the literature the following summary draws the threads of this research together:

> These studies taken together suggest that therapists or counselors who are accurately empathic, non-possessively warm in attitude, and genuine, are indeed effective. Also, these findings seem to hold with a wide variety of therapists and counselors regardless of their training or theoretic orientation and with a wide variety of clients or patients, including college under-achievers, juvenile delinquents, hospitalized schizophrenics, college counsellees, mild to severe outpatients, neurotics, and the mixed variety of hospitalized patients (Truax and Mitchell, 1971, p. 310).

This research evidence also explicitly states that low levels of the 'therapeutic' condition can make the patient 'worse'

(Rogers and Dymond, 1954; Truax and Carkhuff, 1964, 1967; Berenson and Carkhuff, 1967; Carkhuff, 1969, 1971; Truax and Mitchell, 1971). Indeed, it is the difference in these therapeutic levels that partly explains why there is greater variability in the treatment groups versus the control groups in early 'psychotherapy research studies' (Bergin, 1963). In view of the preceding arguments we would claim that 'expectations of outcome' also feature in this 'variability' as they are a central underlying theme of the three characteristics, but more of this discussion in chapter 8.

I think it can be concluded then that the self-fulfilling prophecy model can be applied to client-centred therapy. This approach to helping has not been described here in order to claim that it is 'just a placebo' and should therefore be dismissed. It is not claimed either that the success of Rogerian therapy rests entirely on expectations, since there are many other antecedent and situational therapist and client variables contained in the conditions. The point of this analysis is to demonstrate further how the therapist's original view of the world, and specifically his view of his client's potential, colours his behaviour which in turn produces change in his clients.

Chapter seven

How to maximise the prophet's potency

Status, personality and specific behaviour

The evidence presented so far leads to one inevitable conclusion. The professional helping person must believe in his ability to help the client and in the client's ability to benefit from the change process. This confidence has been stressed by Shapiro who explains that the more intense the belief of the therapist in his treatment, the more impressed will be the patient and the greater his belief. The patient may translate this belief into grounds for his own willingness to rely on the therapist to be helped. However, what is even more important is that the helper displays the type of behaviour which we have seen will be caused by his positive expectations.

Given that the professional helper has 'growth' expectations for his client's future behaviour, and is ready, in his own behaviour, to reinforce that growth in his client, what are the other associated antecedent variables which increase the potency of these prophecies? (We use the term potent prophet to mean experimenters who are 'effective' in communicating bias or influence, and therapists whose prognostic expectations are fulfilled.)

The attempt to relate specific personality characteristics to potent prophets has largely failed. In the same way we have no clear indicators as to what characteristics personify the responsive client. We will see however, that there are notable exceptions to this rather barren picture. Let us survey the state of the market by looking at those areas of research which we used to illustrate the 'importance of expectations'.

Rosenthal investigated the relationship between sex, religion and race of experimenters and subjects but found conflicting results. He was able to show that experimenters with a 'moderate' amount of anxiety seemed to achieve more bias (this is probably related to confidence, see above), but his main positive finding was that high *status* experimenters who displayed an air of 'dominance' and 'professionalism' were likely to have the most effect. There are indications too that likeability, warmth and interest are effective characteristics. (We may remember 'Clever Hans' at this stage—Rosenthal's work has confirmed the findings of Pfungst.) Rosenthal also found that those experimenters who 'liked' their subjects influenced them more (Rosenthal, 1966, 1969).

Barber states in his conclusions that the extent to which the personal characteristics of the experimenter—for example his age, sex, ethnic background and personality—interact with the characteristics of subjects, to affect their behaviour, is not known at this stage. He adds that it is the client's 'attitudes, expectations and motivations with respect to the immediate test-situation, rather than to differences among individuals in enduring personality traits', which influence their test behaviour (Barber, 1969).

However, Barber found that the *status* of the experimenter was important. For example, if an attempt is made by a prestigeful person to produce negative attitudes and expectations in subjects who have previously manifested high response, these subjects now show very little if any response to test-situations of the type traditionally associated with the word hypnosis (Barber, 1969).

Our third area of knowledge—placebo effects—reveals a similar picture, attempts to relate placebo effects to the patient's personality having failed because traits found in one study have not been confirmed in others done under different conditions (Shapiro, 1971). Shapiro, as we have seen in previous chapters, underlines the importance of the helper's interest in the client and also points out the crucial importance of the prestige and status of the therapist.

We are reminded here of the 'Hawthorn Effect' well known in sociology (Roethlisberger and Dickson, 1939) and Frank's finding that the mere introduction of a research team into a veterans' hospital was enough to produce patient improvement (Frank, 1973).

Shapiro also underlines Barber's point that it is the attitudes and expectations that the therapist and client bring to the 'specific' situation which are important rather than continuing personality traits. This he illustrates by indicating that subjects can vary in their placebo response from time to time (Shapiro, 1971).

In the area of psychotherapy research we must first recognise the over-riding importance of accurate empathy, genuineness and non-possessive warmth. We note that both Rosenthal and Shapiro have highlighted characteristics which can be subsumed under those headings (warmth, interest, attention). However, we have already discussed these characteristics in detail and shown their importance as 'reinforcers' in the interaction. What of other characteristics that we can add to these? We should note that we are not attempting to outline further helping characteristics *per se* but only those which are likely to add to the change agent's prophecy potency.

Goldstein confirms Rosenthal's finding that mutual attraction is significantly related to therapist/experimenter influence. He also shows how the therapist's 'authoritarianism', 'confidence' and 'lack of anxiety' enhance the communication of his expectations (Goldstein, 1962).

In chapter 4 we saw some indications of the importance of attraction between therapist and client. We may now add that it has been found that the therapist's feelings and attitudes about the client influence the interaction for better or worse (Strupp, 1958). In a study by Heller and Goldstein it was found that patient attraction was significantly and positively related to the therapist's prognostic expectancy (Heller and Goldstein, 1961; Goldstein, 1973).

However, the most often noted characteristic outlined above, the status of the prophet, is that which seems to be of crucial significance. Frank and others argue that it is the therapist's position in society as 'Healer' which enables him to have influence over his patients (Kiev, 1966; Frank, 1968, 1973; Ehrenwald, 1966; Calestro, 1972). This argument has been succinctly put by Shapiro:

> The prestigious heritage of the priest, scientist, and physician is represented in our culture by the psychotherapist. . . . To him are attributed omniscience, omnipotence, integrity, dedication, and esoteric knowledge. . . . Society's sanction of his role makes him even more prestigious.
>
> Illness is usually stressful . . . familiar cues for integration decrease; ambiguity and stimulus hunger increases . . . and regressive fantasies . . . guilt . . . anxiety . . . depression . . . and dependency . . . are stimulated—all factors that have been cited as correlates of suggestibility and the placebo effect.
>
> The favourable feelings of the therapist have been associated with the increased expression of affect by patients . . . which may further decrease guilt through catharsis. It is also related to increased suggestibility, conditioning, and learning in patients. Patients become suggestible, and are inordinately reassured by the interest of the prestigious therapist . . . (Shapiro, 1971, p. 456).

(Shapiro is of course talking about the USA. When we translate these views to this country we should bear in mind the greater acceptance and status of psychotherapy in that society relative to our own.)

The influence of the expectations of high status prophets is supported by the arguments of labelling theorists. An essential facet of the theory is that a major reason why certain behaviour is labelled deviant is because of the *power* of the labellers. Without this position of power, it is argued, the behaviour would not be so labelled, or, to put it another

71

way, if the power relationships were reversed then so might the labelling of behaviour be. This is best illustrated by fringe activities, such as marihuana smoking, where attitudes and hence the force of the label is gradually changing. One might ask the question—would our attitude toward 'pot' smoking be changed if it was only participated in by a poor, inarticulate, under-privileged minority?

Thus the main characteristics which maximise the prophet's potency are the mutual attraction of prophet and client and the relatively high status of the prophet.

The matching of helper and client expectations

Calestro, in a comparative study of healing methods, argues that the high status of the prophet is important because it perpetuates the shared 'myth', within whatever society it is, that illness, problems and thus cures can be explained by that society's healers. He, like Frank, demonstrates that it is necessary for the helper and client to share definitions, beliefs, assumptions and expectations about healing methods if they are to prove efficacious (Calestro, 1972; Frank, 1973).

This sharing of 'assumptive worlds' can also be illustrated within western society. Goldstein's arguments concerning the 'failure' of most forms of therapy with working- or lower-class clients hinge upon the clash of expectations and beliefs that these clients bring relative to their typically middle-class therapists. He demonstrates that the lower-class patient is far more likely to come to therapy expecting immediate, concrete, active, problem-orientated solutions to problems usually seen as an environmental crisis. These clients are typically met by a therapist who views the cause of problems as internal and the methods of approaching them as long term, general if not abstract, emotive rather than concrete, and his role in their solution relatively passive and at least fairly non-directive. It is not surprising, and a mark perhaps of the 'realism' of lower-class clients, that they often quickly break off contact (Goldstein, 1973).

Coe and Buckner have outlined three general principles which will affect the potency of expectations and related factors: first, the degree to which the therapist's ability to name the problem and its causes agrees with the views of the client; second, the degree to which the therapeutic techniques employed are considered by the client to be of value in helping him; and third the degree to which the therapist's personal qualities match the client's expectations of what a therapist should be like (Coe and Buckner, 1975).

These factors need not be left to chance. Not only can professional helpers actively attempt to match clients to workers along these guidelines but also steps can be taken to vary expectations to match them. The first point is perhaps best illustrated by the 'New Careers' developments. This idea of taking clients who have achieved some progress and training them to help others in similar situations is a direct way of matching the assumptive worlds of worker and client (Carkhuff, 1971). Before we explore the second we should say more about the status of the helper and the clash of expectations on another level. It does not always follow that because the professional helper has high prestige in the society that he will influence the client. In an investigation of the placebo effect carried out by Park and Covi all patients showed improvement except one, this patient did not take the pill because of her husband's views towards it (Park and Covi, 1965). This illustrates that the prophet has to be a significant person for the client. This opens up an area hitherto unexplored.

The client and conflicting expectations

The professional helper is but one person in the client's life. There are of course many others—husbands, wives, children, parents, etc. All will have expectations of the client's behaviour and thus be making implicit or explicit prophecies about how he or she will behave. We cannot assume that the professional helper is going to be the most potent of these nor can we leave the client to be torn by these conflicting expectations. Although we have focused exclusively on the professional helper/client relationship in order to analyse the workings of the interactional mechanisms, we do not mean to imply that this is the sole focus of intervention. In order to take these other expectations into consideration we advocate that the worker must be conscious of, and work with, these other expectations on the client in order to modify, or work with, them and thus increase his own positive prophecy effect. If he ignores them, the confusion and stress caused in the client by interaction may precipitate deterioration in his condition despite the otherwise 'correct' attitudes and behaviour of the change agent. As we shall see in our final chapter this point has important consequences for all agents of change.

The level of expectations

We might assume that the higher the expectations of the therapist the greater their potency but this is not so. Rosenthal found that if his experimenters were deliberately trying to influence their subjects or being tempted to cheat with their results, they actually produced less bias not more (Rosenthal, 1966). Frank also argues that if expectations are too high or too low they will have little effect on treatment outcome. He points out the dangers of allowing the client to expect a magical cure, or blaming him for that expectation, and asserts that it is the responsibility of the therapist to set 'realistic' limits to the treatment process (Frank, 1968, 1973; Betz, 1968).

The reader will remember that the research outlined by Strupp in chapter 4 found that those therapists with 'non-committal' (as opposed to high or low) expectations tended to offer the highest therapeutic levels (Strupp, 1960). Goldstein tested this and found that there was a 'curvilinear relationship' between expected and perceived change. That is to say moderate prognostic expectations report the greatest symptom reduction; extreme prognostic expectations report minimal symptom reduction (Goldstein, 1962).

If we apply our model of the self-fulfilling prophecy to these findings we can perhaps explain them. If the initial prophecy is too high, no amount of intervention—in terms of possible behaviour—will bring about change in the direction of the prophecy. Thus 'unrealistic' expectations may be taken to mean expectations which cannot be fulfilled by the possible behaviour range of the change agent. If the initial prophecy is too low then the reinforcing type behaviour will not be geared to effect any significant change at all. If low-positive expectations are read as being negative expectations a harmful self-fulfilling prophecy may be set in motion.

We should note here that the range of client conditions amenable to change through a 'personal' relationship has its limitations. One would obviously not expect to be able to modify the effects of brain damage for example. However, the distinction between psychological and physical illness is becoming increasingly hazy as more conditions are shown to have a psychosomatic component (Schmale, 1969). We shall also bear in mind that evidence which has claimed physiological change as a result of non-medical treatment processes (Frank, 1973; Sargent, 1957), and the work of Platonov, based on Pavlov's theories, claims that 'words' can be used to change physiological states in the mind (Platonov, 1959). We should also note that probably all physical disorders have an indirect if not direct psychological component as suggested by placebo research (Platonov, 1959; Beecher, 1961; Shapiro, 1971).

Setting optimum conditions

Let us now return to the steps the professional helper can take to vary the expectations of the client and match his own to them. We can now see that this needs to be done not only with shared assumptions of problems and their solution but also on the level of expectations of change.

Several writers have discussed the value of role-induction interviews either by negotiating what is likely to happen or actually to demonstrate, with video-taped interviews, a therapy session. These attempts have had some success in improving the direction and thus outcome of therapy (Truax and Carkhuff, 1967; Frank, 1973; Goldstein, 1973).

Goldstein, in his book *Structural Learning Therapy,* takes this approach further by arguing for and then demonstrating a method of treatment specifically designed to match the strategy of intervention to the characteristics, including expectations, of the client group (Goldstein, 1973).

Thus we have seen in this chapter, that given a professional change agent who is able to bring a fairly high level of accurate empathy, genuineness and non-possessive warmth to a relationship, and has positive expectations towards his client's growth and the outcome of the relationship, his status and the mutual attraction between him and the client are additional important variables affecting his helping potency.

The need for the professional worker to involve himself with all other members of the client system because (a) the change agent is but one person who is making (implicit or explicit) prophecies about the client's future and (b) because the personal significance, prestige and status of the helper, in the eyes of the client (i.e. where in the phenomenological world of the client does the professional helper rank) is of crucial importance. The helper may have to work with, or effectively and consciously against, the expectations which others in the client's life have of him.

The optimum level of expectations, for both worker and client, is a moderate, 'realistic' one; expectations that are too high or too low are at best ineffective, at worst harmful.

Finally, we should underline the reservation that in order for self-fulfilling prophecies to work the prophet's behaviour has to be capable of bringing about the expected change in the client; that is there are conditions where no matter what the therapist expects, his behaviour is unable to do anything about it, or bring about change in the time expected by the client.

Chapter eight

For better or for worse

A common assumption made by members of the helping professions is that their efforts either help or have no effect. This chapter challenges that assumption and discusses the role which expectations may play in the 'for better, for worse argument'. At various stages in our discussions we have referred to this controversy and the research findings which relate to it. Now let us look at the arguments in more detail.

The debate reviewed

Eysenck's series of articles have challenged the effects of psychotherapy, counselling and such methods of intervention. By a detailed statistical analysis of a variety of studies he argues that in total the evidence they present suggests that therapy is no better than spontaneous remission, in other words the clients that improved would have improved without any 'help' (Eysenck, 1952, 1960, 1965). These papers have had a significant effect upon the area of therapy research and have thrown down the gauntlet to members of the helping professions to demonstrate that they were not wasting their time.

Cartwright and later Bergin looked hard at these outcome studies and noticed that although the *average* improvement was similar between therapy and non-therapy groups there was a significantly greater variation in the treated patients. This, it is argued, implies that some patients must have shown significantly greater improvement while others could only maintain the overall average by showing a greater deterioration (Cartwright, 1955; Bergin, 1963).

While this debate over the interpretation of other people's findings was going on a series of research projects was under way which was to provide significant evidence in the debate. Carl Rogers and others had already identified the value of empathy, warmth and genuineness and were now testing these therapist characteristics in a major study at Wisconsin University. Preliminary findings indicated that some types of therapists did better than others. But these findings had a sting in the tail. *Some therapists seemed to make their patients worse!!* (Rogers and Dymond, 1954; Rogers, 1967.)

These findings were replicated in repeated studies in different settings by Truax and Carkhuff who also demonstrated that the results were directly related to the therapist's characteristics. That is, where the therapist demonstrated high levels of non-passive warmth, genuineness and empathy the outcome of therapy was successful but where the therapist demonstrated low levels of these characteristics clients were actually seen to *deteriorate!!* (Truax and Carkhuff, 1967.)

These findings led to another paper by Bergin drawing some of these findings together. One of his conclusions was that most forms of psychotherapy make patients worse as well as better and this accounts for the lack of difference in the average improvement found in so many studies between treated patients and controls (Bergin, 1966). It was also being argued that 'controls' did not necessarily mean 'untreated'. That there are a variety of people to whom these clients could turn for help though not receiving help from the professional therapists. As has been pointed out by Truax and Carkhuff there is absolutely no reason to suppose that professionals have a monopoly on the 'helping characteristics', and indeed there are indications that lay helpers may be more effective (Bergin, 1966; Truax and Carkhuff, 1967; Carkhuff, 1969; Carkhuff, 1971; Frank, 1973; Goldstein, 1973). It has been suggested that this finding occurs because lay helpers are chosen for their personality characteristics, while professional helpers are selected according to academic ability (Carkhuff, 1969).

But, of course, these were not the last words and Eysenck again returned to the attack. But in 1971 Bergin re-examined much of the relevant research literature again, this time indicating that Eysenck had overestimated the 'spontaneous remission' findings and underestimated those which showed therapy to be effective. Bergin maintained his position on the for better, for worse debate reviewing some thirty-one studies which had shown a deterioration effect (Eysenck, 1967; Bergin, 1971).

Now Rachman (1971) took up Eysenck's part in the argument and criticised Bergin's statistics, while May (1971) also pointed to weaknesses in the greater variation argument and some of the 'deterioration' findings. Thus some doubts have been thrown on the evidence in individual studies but as Malan has pointed out the overall evidence has an essentially cumulative effect. We should also point out that the criticisms fail to take into consideration all of the evidence of the deterioration effect presented in the literature (Truax and Carkhuff, 1967; Carkhuff, 1969, 1971; Malan, 1973; Egan, 1975).

Bergin (1975) has reasserted his position in a provocative article in which he refers to evidence that group as well as individual therapy can be harmful. He gives several examples of how harm can be caused. He analyses a series of studies which cover various types of therapy and include nearly one thousand cases from delinquent youths to hospitalised schizophrenics. He concludes that the results indicate that 65 per cent of those who received therapy get better, compared to only 40 per cent who improve without formal treatment. Thus it would seem that at least 25 per cent show progress as a result of the therapist's intervention. But, again he concludes that intervention causes harm. He found that 10 per cent of treated clients deteriorated compared to 5 per cent in non-treatment control groups, thus indicating that intervention can be fairly blamed for the additional 5 per cent in the former group.

For better or for worse

It should be remembered that in the opening chapter we pointed out the irrelevance of treating psychotherapy etc. as a unitary phenomenon. Much of the research quoted, which demonstrates the deterioration effect and the value of therapy, is based on actual observation of interactors, rating the therapist's behaviour and relating it to outcome. The Eysenck, Rachman, May position, however, is based on an overall statistical analysis of the data.

On balance, then, it would seem that the weight of the cumulative research evidence lends greater support to an assumption that therapy could be 'for better or for worse' than it does to the assumption that it is 'helpful or has no effect', or even 'that it has no effect at all'. In addition to the evidence presented in the above debate, others have warned of the dangers of intervention by professional helpers. The supporters of the New Careers projects have illustrated how professional helpers can impoverish their clients and maintain them in a state of suspended dependency (Hodgkin, 1973).

But the warnings of help turning sour are not monopolised by new and more 'radical' approaches to therapy. Freud, for example, wrote in 1912: 'The outbreak of negative transference is a very common occurrence in institutions; as soon as he is seized by it the patient leaves, uncured or worse' (p. 113), and in 1910 he devoted an article to 'Observations on "Wild" Psychoanalysis', in which he warned against glib, simplistic interpretations which might harm rather than help treatment (see Freud, 1963).

Let us then take a closer look at the 'no effect or help' assumption. Why do professionals assume that their interaction can do no harm? It is not hard to understand why people who have undergone training which is not only time consuming but often involves a high degree of personal involvement and emotional upheaval, even pain, will be loth to admit that at the end of it all they are no better at achieving their goal than before they started. It has, after all, long been recognised that the more difficult and painful the initiation rights into a particular group the greater the loyalty and identification of members once accepted. If we add to these considerations our natural needs to meet personal failure with denial, we see that helpers are possibly highly motivated to avoid facing up to possible negative consequences of their efforts. So the assumption persists, often even among those who are sceptical or even cynical of the efforts of professional helpers, preferring to assume impotence than admit that harm is a possible outcome of intervention.

But where is the evidence that human interaction has a built in fail-safe mechanism which dictates that harm cannot be done by the interaction of one person to another? Put like that it is surely obvious that unfortunately such fail-safe mechanisms do not exist. Ironically, the situation is that professional helpers will attribute the cause of many of their client's difficulties to the effects of previous interactions with significant people in the client's lives. If we accept that interaction between others and our clients can adversely affect them it surely applies to us too.

Helpful and harmful prophets

What has the central hypothesis of this book to contribute to this debate? We have demonstrated in previous chapters that the expectations of the change agent can influence outcome as illustrated by the self-fulfilling prophecy model. Our discussion of self-fulfilling prophecies clearly shows that these expectations can be in any direction, their limitation being caused by the limitations of the effect of one person's behaviour on another. Therefore, unless we do assume that one person's behaviour cannot harm another, it follows that the therapist's self-fulfilling prophecies can be harmful if his expectations are negative or stunting. The covert, implicit nature of some self-fulfilling prophecies suggests that often neither helper nor helpee is aware of the process in operation. This conclusion can also be reached by reflecting on the evidence presented which demonstrates the different quality of behaviour different expectations seem to precipitate, and the relationship between these different qualities and outcome. As we have seen above high levels of warmth, empathy, genuineness etc. lead to positive change whereas low levels lead to negative outcome.

Thus we can conclude that expectations significantly influence whether the intervention of the professional helper will be for better or for worse.

But we saw above that considerable doubt had been cast on whether control groups in therapy research were really 'no treatment' groups. That is they received the help of lay people. Why then are these findings not equally variable, that is why are they not equally made better or worse by laymen? Again our analysis may indicate part of the answer. The description of the potent prophet deduced from the evidence in chapter 7 suggests that the professional helper, with his position and status recognised by society and the client, may indeed be more potent than the layman, thus his expectations, for better or for worse, may be likely to have more effect.

We can now return to our brief discussion of labelling theory and again illustrate its interrelationship with our hypothesis. The evidence supporting the self-fulfilling prophecy hypothesis does indicate that the types of mechanisms described by labelling theorists can indeed take place. Labelling theory has, in the main, described how these processes have placed and confirmed people in their role as deviants. We should again emphasise that the extent to which the label will 'stick' and precipitate future behaviour consistent with the label will depend in part on the strength of the implied prophecy of future behaviour.

The professional helper may play a crucial role in the deviant's career, be he 'delinquent' or 'mentally ill'. It will be remembered that Becker and others use the concept of the deviant career to describe the stages of a person becoming an outsider. Crucial to proceeding from being labelled and passing on into further deviancy was the acceptance of the deviant status as master status, that is, it is as a deviant that the individual is primarily known.

Consider then the function performed by the professional helper who has somebody who has been caught committing their first deviant act referred to him. I suggest there is a tendency for this person to be described almost totally in terms of that deviant act. Information will be collected, and reported, in order to make sense of that act, and the many other facets of the person, the other roles he plays, all too easily overlooked. More will be said of these dangers in the final chapter.

The way in which implicit expectations can trap clients in a stunting self-fulfilling prophecy is startingly illustrated in the following example; part of a letter written by Jung to Freud which was a factor in the split between the two men:

> I would, however, point out that your technique of treating your pupils like patients is a BLUNDER. In that way you produce either slavish sons or impudent puppies. . . . I am objective enough to see through your little trick. You go around sniffing out all the symptomatic actions in your vicinity, thus reducing everyone to the level of sons and daughters who blushingly admit the existence of their faults. Meanwhile you remain on top as the father, sitting pretty. For sheer obsequiousness nobody dares to pluck the prophet by the beard and inquire for once what you would say to a patient with a tendency to analyse the analyst instead of himself. You would certainly ask him: "Who's got the neurosis?" (Jung, 1974, letter 338 J).

We might well ask if it is a good way to treat patients?

Outcome and choice

The discussion on the effectiveness of helping relationships may well have overlooked one very important point in assuming that a 100 per cent 'success' finding is a worthy goal for the helping professions to achieve. This assumption overlooks the full significance of therapy as a method of influence and persuasion. We saw in chapter 5 that the evidence suggests that a 'non-directive' stance was not, in practice, possible. This, of course, is particularly true if we are considering bringing about changes in behaviour which are often defined by others as in need of change, rather than the client. Now if we view the helping professions as having a monopoly on the truth we might justifiably look for a 100 per cent success rating. This will also be a legitimate goal if we regard the client as having no power of choice. But we know that these professions do not have a monopoly on truth; they cannot because they have so many internal contradictions and disagreements. Then it may be entirely 'healthy' that the client 'fails' to respond to treatment.

You will remember that in our opening chapter we suggested that a core activity in the helping professions was that they offered the clients *alternatives*, an alternative strategy, alternative view of the world, alternative understanding of themselves, alternative view of themselves, etc. Now if we build this into our assessment of the 'success' of intervention we might see that 100 per cent success is highly unlikely and undesirable. If one of the goals of the helping relationship is that the change agent offers a constructive and realistic alternative *modus operandi* to the client then his success should be judged on the appropriateness of the alternative and its presentation to the client. But not necessarily on *whether the client accepts that alternative*. The client might reject the alternative presented by the professional helper. *He has that choice.* Client self-determination is a reality, not something we allow him—he has it if he chooses to take it. If one doubts this, explain why so many do not respond to the coercive influences in society—indeed our clients often are 'clients' just because they demonstrate their self-determination despite the conforming pressures of the social institutions around them. Surely this is one of the messages of Solzhenitsyn's book *A Day in the Life of Ivan Denisovich,* and for that matter, Solzhenitsyn's own history; that no matter what pressures, the will is not destroyed and the choice not to conform can always be made if an alternative is recognised.

Thus it is apparent that, unless we want professional helpers to be those who put 1984 into practice, we should not judge them on what their clients decide to do but only on how they have helped the client understand his predicament and have opened up alternative ways of approaching its solution. The dilemma presented by the self-fulfilling prophecy hypothesis is that unless the change agent makes a prediction that the client will be able to make decisions for himself, there is a danger that the client might accept the other expectations of the therapist unaware that other alternatives may be open to him and that some of these other expectations may be equally stunting.

Chapter nine

Prophecy and practice

The main conclusion reached is that there is cumulative evidence from various fields of research which supports the central hypothesis, that the expectations of professional helpers can be self-fulfilling prophecies and thus affect outcome.

In chapter 1 we emphasised that the worker's expectations are but one variable among several which will influence the course and outcome of any relationship which will bring about change. This means that even if expectations are at optimum levels other variables may intervene to alter the course of therapy. However, that does not alter our conclusion that expectations themselves may be very important and affect outcome for better and for worse. Any factor in intervention is bound to have its limitations and we have seen that as expectations are mediated through the behaviour of the change agent their effect is limited by the amount of change that that behaviour can bring about.

The evidence presented here is deduced from a variety of sources and, with the exception of the Pygmalion research and Goldstein's work on prognostic expectations, has not been designed to test the self-fulfilling prophecy type hypothesis *per se*. It seems crucial, therefore, to test this hypothesis directly, especially considering the seriousness of the possible implications. This research, it is suggested, should be based on three main areas: first on the relationship between expectations, behaviour and outcome so as to provide further evidence to confirm or modify the hypothesis;

second, on the actual reciprocal behaviour so as to understand more about the moment-by-moment interaction, thus
confirming or disproving our speculations as to how
prophecies are communicated; and finally to investigate
further the characteristics of the potent prophet and the
receptive client so that the influence of appropriate
prophecies can be maximised—and inappropriate ones
minimised.

In chapter 8 attention was drawn to the difficult and
complex area of the assessment of outcome of helping
relationships. It was suggested that the quality of the
alternative strategy and/or view of the world offered by the
therapist to the client should be a focus of assessment. Thus
change agents would be assessed on their ability to present
appropriate alternatives in a way which enables their clients
to make realistic choices.

The importance of the expectations of the professional
helper, as the agent of change, and as a model for the client,
strongly suggests that we should take the optimism and
'hope' of students into account when selecting them for
training. We also endorse the view that therapist ability to
solve problems personally will be a crucial factor if we are
not going to set up a 'blind leading the blind' situation when
we attempt to help clients. After all, the belief that an
alternative is available leads one to search for it and maybe
find it. Is it likely that people will search for an alternative
they do not believe is there?

The potential power of expectations to fulfil themselves
through the behaviour of those engaged in attempting to
help and bring about change in people makes it imperative
for change agents to be aware of what their prophecies
really are. We have seen that the action of self-fulfilling
prophecies can be covert, implicit and subtle and easily
disguised from the helper and helped alike. We have also
seen that they can be for better or for worse. Thus, there is a
need for the change agent to expect positive change in his
client. If we take into consideration that the likelihood of
therapists holding this view is correlated with the mutual

attraction between helper and client we can see that this is a powerful argument to support those views regarding therapist/client matching.

In a perfect world the client would be matched to the professional helper who liked him and firmly believed that he could help to develop the potential in the client. However, many workers, be they agency based social workers, doctors or psychiatrists, cannot choose their clients any more than clients can choose their professional helpers. It becomes a necessity, therefore, that change agents broaden their understanding of all types of clients so that they can 'like them all' and recognise, even in the most unfortunate amongst them, potential for growth and change. We are not faced with a situation where we can say 'this one I will help but that one must stop as he is'. Our statutory obligations often require us to work with them all and those we do *not* have positive expectations of *WE MAY MAKE WORSE!!*

At the beginning and during the relationship it is necessary to work towards an appropriate level of expectations with the client. Modifying those that are either too high or too low. This will be a necessary first step in many situations. If the client does not expect to be helped our conclusions indicate he will not gain by the relationship until hope is aroused. During the relationship it is necessary to keep check on these expectations that they neither wane nor grow beyond the bounds of immediate possibility. The writer is conscious here of suggesting that the change agent walks a tight-rope on which he frankly realises the difficulty of balancing. However, it is necessary to understand what level of optimistic expectations are 'realistic' for the individual client in treatment and the writer's own inclination would be to be on the side of expecting too much rather than risk the stunting effect of expecting too little or nothing at all.

The need for the client to come to treatment with 'realistic' expectations and the need for status and prestige all suggest that the helping professions need a skilful and effective public relations job done to 'sell' the optimum image to the public, i.e. the potential clientele. One suspects at present that many client expectations of social workers are too low and of psychiatrists, too high, but this is little more than a hunch. Accurate 'market research' needs to be done to find out just what people's expectations are before we attempt change of expectations on the macro scale.

We might also add that expectations about those who deal with emotional and behavioural problems are unrealistic in another sense. If one goes to the doctor one does not expect him to provide a cure that will ensure that you never go to him again. It is recognised that the body is a complex organism vulnerable to a variety of conditions. One expects, and normally gets, help with a specific problem from a doctor, but neither doctor nor patient anticipate that this is the last time they see each other.

Our attitude toward emotional, social and behavioural problems, however, is far more simplistic. Often social workers, psychiatrists, psychotherapists, etc. are judged on 'remission' rates. That implies that they are expected to effect a one time cure, and that if a person receives help for emotional, social or psychological problems then 'successful treatment' will mean that it will not be necessary to go to see that professional helper again.

I suggest our emotional, psychological and social lives far from being simple are as complex as our physical organism and just as vulnerable to a variety of conditions. Ironically many of these problems are considered incurable, a reaction, I suggest, to us expecting too much in the first place and now, hopes dashed, expecting little or nothing. These assumptions are also probably based on the large amount of psychological literature which has focused on the 'growth and development' of people and related this to 'problems'. Thus, once 'mature', help in these areas should not be needed, intervention is then geared at 'maturing' people so that they will be independent thereafter. I do not mean to deny the crucial importance of past and upbringing, but merely to question these assumptions. After all many of our clients who seem to be reasonably mature need help. The physical body does not react in this way, tending to need more 'help' as it gets older. If man is influenced by 'aims' as well as 'causes' how does death influence his social, emotional and psychological life?

What I am suggesting then is that professional helpers and their clients can have reasonable expectations of the former being able to help the latter with problems and difficulties in the social and psychological aspects of their lives. But that expectations which are too high, as we have seen, will lead only to disillusionment and failure, and eventually no expectation of help which will produce the same result.

On the micro scale we have seen the value of pre-therapy induction procedures. It seems this is an important way in which expectations can be modified to optimum level. It also underlines the need for continued negotiation between worker and client about what is and is not possible as a result of their interaction.

We saw that it is essential for the professional helper to have confidence and faith in his own abilities and the client's potential for change. Thus it becomes more and more important that the professional change agent gains, from his professional colleagues, reinforcement of the belief that his expectations of himself and his clients are 'realistic'. The helping professions are indeed as Halmos has said, professions which 'declare for hope' (Halmos, 1965, p. 6).

The role of supervision in social work should be mentioned here. There is a temptation to go along with the depression and frustration caused by some clients in any worker, and take a 'realistic' line. One then might 'reassure' the worker that 'nobody could be expected to help that particular person' etc. In my experience this rarely helps—officially accepted impotence is not much easier to bear than private failure. Also it is rarely very 'realistic'—the worker will often 'battle on' regardless and in fact there are few situations in which one cannot do 'something', no matter how small, to effect some relief or some small change. One can go on offering alternatives even if the client does choose to ignore them. More often, I suggest, this 'hopelessness' is the product of too high, too grand, expectations backfiring. It may be true that a total change of personality, behaviour, circumstances, is not possible in the foreseeable future, but all people are changing and small modifications can be attempted and be reasonably expected to happen. A small change may provide positive feedback to the client which promotes a subsequent larger change. In this way the client may begin to reconstrue the possibilities open to him, that is to say, begin making positive self-fulfilling prophecies about his own future.

In our opening chapter we put forward the case that if our hypothesis was found to be supported by evidence then this would lend weight to the labelling theorists' position, inasmuch as it would demonstrate that the mechanisms they described actually can be set in motion by the implicit expectation in a label. We also noted that in many of the labels they mention, 'schizophrenic', 'drug addict', 'delinquent', etc. there often is an implied prophecy commonly accepted that these people will continue to behave in a deviant way. In the last chapter we noted how the professional helper might contribute, harmfully, to this process by further confirming the label on his client. Before offering suggestions as to how this might be avoided let us look at another aspect of professional intervention that raises similar problems.

It has often seemed apparent to the writer that we are reasonably good at 'understanding', or at least analysing, the clients' problems but not always so good at doing anything about them. Based on the conclusions noted above we tentatively suggest a reason for, and maybe a way of changing, this state of affairs.

At the beginning of the book we suggested that it aimed at shifting the focus of intervention from the past to the future; let us outline our case.

We have seen that expectations held by the therapist and the client can influence their behaviour in their interaction and that self-fulfilling prophecies are set in motion. That is

91

to say, how the therapist and the client see the latter's future will be a crucial antecedent variable in what it becomes.

There is a danger in focusing on the client's past and on the symptoms of his present distress. Although we realise the importance of discussing and allowing the client to express his feelings about them, we must be careful that we do not reinforce the client in his problems. We must be careful that we do not show him acceptance, genuineness and accurate empathy only when he is reporting his pathology and thus perpetuate rather than relieve his present and past crises.

In fact we tend to look for previous traumas, deprivations and problems in order that we can build an acceptable hypothesis based on patterns in this pathology, to explain the present situation. We take social histories, often records of things that went wrong, and look for signs of conflict and disruption in the individual and in his interaction with his immediate and wider social system. We pay lip service to looking at '*strengths* and weaknesses', but how often do we see a list of healthy attributes and adaptive skills in a social history?

Out of this pathology-based information we attempt to build a treatment plan. This seems analogous to trying to rebuild a house out of the rotting timbers that caused it to collapse!!

We look at the 'milestones' in a child's development but often only those that were stumbling blocks, the others seem to slip past unnoticed. And there is a clue—pathology seems to be more interesting, more prominent than health, as the front page of any newspaper will testify.

But it is by understanding the strengths and positive personality characteristics of the client that we, as change agents, can come to expect growth and positive change in him. Often these strengths lie in those acts which might otherwise be described as symptoms of the client's 'pathology'. Consider the so-called 'inadequate' person who 'manipulates' the social-security system. His 'manipulation' is seen as part of his symptomatology, but, it is also the way in which he adapts to the system. It is *his* way, often pretty effective, of coping with his situation. Often such a client displays considerable knowledge, effort, cunning and perseverence. That change in this client's behaviour is 'desirable' may be so but that it is a symptom of 'inadequacy' is often completely wrong.

It is these potentialities in him that we wish to reinforce with our expectations and behaviour, so that they may develop and overtake the negative, pathological aspects. We have seen the power of such a positive view of the client's potential in our discussion of client-centred therapy as a self-fulfilling prophecy.

It is in this way that, I suggest, the professional helper can combat the course of a deviant career and be an antidote rather than a contributing factor in the labelling process. The labelling process, of course, presents wider issues than just that concerning the helping professions and reminds us that the professional change agent is not the only prophet in the client's life. Thus he will have to be involved in working on the expectations of those other potent prophets in the client's family, work, school or wider social network. He will also have to be involved, in an even wider sense, in attempting to influence the labellers who are, we should remember, often those with power. Not that I am necessarily advocating changing the rules in society. But the self-fulfilling prophecy hypothesis points out that where the label implies a prediction of future deviancy it may set in motion processes which precipitate more rule breaking on the part of the affected individuals. Thus if the incidence of deviant behaviour is to be affected so must be this prediction and the behaviour precipitated by it.

At the time of writing there is a current issue which illustrates these problems. Difficulties of placing 'juvenile delinquents' in suitable institutions are currently experienced by social workers and courts. This is presumed to be caused by the changes put into effect following the 1969 Children and Young Persons Act when the approved-school system was integrated into the community homes run by local authorities who do not *have* to accept all children referred. Thus many juvenile offenders, who would previously have been 'contained' are in fact living at home and presumed to be causing problems by continuing to offend. Now, obviously, this is a complex and controversial area and its causes and the exact nature of the problem are hard to ascertain. I do not propose to go into these in depth and this version of the chain of events is given because it is one commonly argued and not because I have evidence that it is the most likely explanation.

I have referred to this debate because many magistrates, police officers and others, including social workers, are claiming that we should 'identify the hard core of offenders' and deal with them separately in closed conditions as opposed to the more liberal set of alternatives open at present to other offenders. Now it seems to me that this is just the sort of situation we have been discussing. Implied, and often openly declared, is the prediction that this 'hard core' are tomorrow's 'professional criminals', the day after's 'recidivists' and presumably eventually next century's 'inadequate ex-offenders'.

Now these might be true predictions; they will almost certainly be in danger of being self-fulfilling prophecies if we do isolate these individuals and treat them on the assumption that they will offend again and again. But if it is a true prediction, if containment is necessary, and many will argue both, do we have to take the risk of fulfilling our own prophecies?

My answer to this is that we have shown that outcome is dependent upon *behaviour* precipitated by the prophecy, not on the belief itself. Thus, if we can be sure that having identified these individuals we can help to bring about change in the course of their deviant careers, that is, if we are convinced that we can behave in a way that does not confirm the prophecy, that is turn it into an anti-self-fulfilling prophecy, then we should proceed with the strategy. This will, of course, mean that other significant people's expectations and thus behaviour will have to change too, if the scheme is to work. This will not happen by accident but only after a hard uphill struggle by professional helpers. If we are not sure that we can overcome the negative self-fulfilling prophecy effect we are probably best advised not to identify these 'hard core' individuals for it could well make them worse.

In the opening chapter I explained that my focus was going to be on the behaviour of change agents rather than their intellectual theories. The evidence referred to has, I think, confirmed the necessity of this focus. As we have seen it is the *behaviour* stage of the self-fulfilling prophecy which precipitates change, not just the belief itself. We draw attention to this area because our goal is to improve the reliability of the helping professions. Thus by understanding the link between expectations, behaviour and outcome we might learn more about how to control our *behaviour* in our interactions with clients.

The next stage is to be able to *behave* in a way which produces positive outcome, and is consistent with positive expectations, *consistently,* and eradicate negative outcome precipitated behaviour. Not, it is suggested, by just manipulating expectations, though the need for genuineness suggests this is desirable, but by the professional helper gaining fuller awareness and control over his behaviour.

It follows from this that making the professional helper aware of how he is actually behaving should be a central feature of training. In previous chapters we have noted the discrepancy between theory and practice and the importance of behaviour characteristics generally and how it is evidence about the empathy, warmth and genuineness of change agents which contributes to their helping or harming clients. All of these factors support this focus. If we add to these the somewhat disappointing findings of Bergin and Strupp, that in fact many research workers find that even their own research does not greatly alter their practice, it too adds weight to this focus (Bergin and Strupp, 1972). Egan has shown some of the practical implications of this approach in his book emphasising that cognitive development is only relevant in as much as it affects practice (Egan, 1975).

Thus we may conclude that there are important implications to be drawn from our conclusion that expectations can become Self-Fulfilling Prophecies.

To summarise, we can see that the change agent must focus on his own behaviour as an essential part of the interaction between himself and his client, that the future should be a focus of his intervention and that he needs to identify and build on the client's strengths, avoiding reinforcing previous pathology. He needs to be aware of his expectations and how they influence his behaviour because his prophecy may be self-fulfilling and for better or for worse.

Bibliography

ABERCROMBIE, M. L. J. (1969), *The Anatomy of Judgement*, Penguin Books, Harmondsworth.

ALLPORT, G. W. (1950), 'The Role of Expectancy', chapter 2 of *Tensions that Cause Wars*, ed. H. Cantril, University of Illinois Press, Urbana, Illinois.

BANDURA, A. (1971), 'Psychotherapy Based Upon Modeling Principles', chapter 17 in Bergin and Garfield (1971).

BANNISTER, D. and FRANSELLA, F. (1971), *Inquiring Man*, Penguin Books, Harmondsworth.

BARBER, T. X. (1969), *Hypnosis*, Van Nostrand Reinhold, New York.

BECKER, H. S. (1963), *Outsiders*, Free Press, New York and London, rev. edn 1973.

BEECHER, H. K. (1961), 'Surgery as Placebo', *Journal of the American Medical Association*, vol. 179, pp. 437-40. See Rosenthal and Jacobson (1968), p. 18.

BEECHER, H. K. (1966), 'Pain: One Mystery Solved', *Science*, vol. 151, pp. 840-1. See Rosenthal and Jacobson (1968), p. 18.

BERENSON, B. G. and CARKHUFF, R. R. (1967), *Counseling and Psychotherapy*, Holt, Rinehart & Winston, New York.

BERGIN, A. E. (1963), 'Negative Results Revisited', pp. 47-55 in Berenson and Carkhuff (1967).

BERGIN, A. E. (1964), 'Some Implications of Psychotherapy Research for Therapeutic Practice', pp. 401-21 in Berenson and Carkhuff (1967).

BERGIN, A. E. (1966), 'Some Implications of Psychotherapy Research for Therapeutic Practice', *Journal of Abnormal Psychology*, vol. 71, pp. 235-46.

BERGIN, A. E. (1971), 'The Evaluation of Therapeutic Outcomes', chapter 7 in Bergin and Garfield (1971).

BERGIN, A. E. (1975), 'When Shrinks Hurt: Psychotherapy Can Be Dangerous', *Psychology Today*, vol. 19, no. 6, pp. 96-104.

BERGIN, A. E. and GARFIELD SOL, L. (eds) (1971), *Handbook of Psychotherapy and Behavior Change*, John Wiley, New York.

BERGIN, A. E. and STRUPP, H. H. (1972), *Changing Frontiers in the Science of Psychotherapy*, Aldine-Atherton, Chicago and New York.

BETZ, B. J. (1962), 'Experiences in Research in Psychotherapy with Schizophrenic Patients', in *Research in Psychotherapy*, vol. 11, ed. H. H. Strupp and L. Luborsky, American Psychology Association, Washington, D.C.

Bibliography

BETZ, B. J. (1968), 'Passive Expectations and Infantile Aims', *International Journal of Psychiatry*, vol. 5, pp. 396-7.

BROWN, F. (1968), 'Bereavement and Lack of a Parent in Childhood', chapter 7 of *Foundations of Child Psychiatry*, ed. E. Miller, Pergamon Press, London.

CALESTRO, K. M. (1972), 'Psychotherapy, Faith, Healing and Suggestion', *International Journal of Psychiatry*, vol. 10, pp. 83-113.

CARKHUFF, R. R. (1969), *Helping and Human Relations Vol. II*, Holt, Rinehart and Winston, New York.

CARKHUFF, R. R. (1971), *The Development of Human Resources*, Holt, Rinehart and Winston, New York.

CARTWRIGHT, D. S. (1955), 'Effectiveness of Psychotherapy: A Critique of the Spontaneous Remission Argument', *Journal of Counseling Psychology*, vol. 2, pp. 290-6.

CARTWRIGHT, D. S. and CARTWRIGHT, R. D. (1958), 'Faith and Improvement in Psychotherapy', *Journal of Counseling Psychology*, vol. 5, pp. 174-7.

CARTWRIGHT, R. D. (1961), 'The Effects of Psychotherapy: A Replication and Extension', *Journal of Consulting Psychology*, vol. 25, pp. 376-82. (Also chapter 14 in Berenson and Carkhuff (1967)).

CHAIKIN, A. L., SIGLER, E. and DERLEGA, V. J. (1974), 'Nonverbal Mediators of Teacher Expectancy Effects', *Journal of Personal Social Psychology*, vol. 30, no. 1, pp. 144-9.

CHANCE, E. (1959), *Families in Treatment*, Basic Books, New York. See Goldstein (1962), pp. 64-5.

CHAVES, J. F. (1968), 'Hypnosis reconceptualized: An Overview of Barber's Theoretical and Empirical Work', *Psychological Reports*, vol. 22, pp. 587-608.

CLARK, A. D. B. (1968), 'Problems in Assessing the Later Effects of Early Learning', chapter 4 of *Foundations of Child Psychiatry*, ed. E. Miller, Pergamon Press, London.

COE, W. C. and BUCKNER, L. G. (1975), 'Expectation, Hypnosis and Suggestion Methods', chapter 12 of *Helping People Change*, ed. F. M. Kanfer and A. P. Goldstein, Pergamon Press, London.

COLM, H. (1966), *The Existentialist Approach to Psychotherapy with Adults and Children*, Grune & Stratton, New York.

COOPER, D. (1970), *Psychiatry and Anti-Psychiatry*, Paladin, London.

DRAYER, C. S. (1956), *Disaster Fatigue*, American Psychiatry Association, Committee on Civil Defense, see Goldstein (1962), p. 40.

EGAN, G. (1975), *The Skilled Helper*, Brooke-Cole, Montrey, California.

EHRENWALD, J. (1966), *Psychotherapy: Myth and Method*, Grune & Stratton, New York.

ERIKSON, E. H. (1965), *Childhood and Society*, Penguin Books, Harmondsworth.

EYSENCK, H. J. (1952), 'The Effects of Psychotherapy: An Evaluation', *Journal of Consulting Psychology*, vol. 16, pp. 319-24.

EYSENCK, H. J. (1960), *The Effects of Psychotherapy, Handbook of Abnormal Psychology*, ed. H. J. Eysenck, Pitman Medical, London, p. 697.

EYSENCK, H. J. (1965), 'The Effects of Psychotherapy', *International Journal of Psychiatry*, vol. 1, pp. 99-144.

Bibliography

EYSENCK, H. J. (1967), 'The Non-Professional Psychotherapist', *International Journal of Psychiatry*, vol. 3, pp. 150-3.

FARLEY, F. H. (1972), Correspondence to *British Journal of Social and Clinical Psychology*, vol. II, part I, February 1972.

FIEDLER, F. E. (1950), 'A Comparison of Therapeutic Relationships in Psychoanalytic, Non-Directive and Adlerian Therapy', *Journal of Consulting Psychology*, vol. 14, pp. 436-45.

FIEDLER, F. E. (1953), 'Quantitative Studies on the Role of the Therapist's Feelings Toward their Patients', *Psychotherapy: Theory and Research*, Donald Press, New York, p. 296-315.

FISHER, S., COLE, J. O., RICKELS, K. and UHLENHUTH, E. H. (1964), 'Drug-Set Interaction: The Effect of Expectations on Drug Response in Out-Patients', *Neuro-Psychopharmacology*, vol. 3, ed. P. B. Bradley, F. Flugel and P. Hock, Elsevier, New York, pp. 149-56. See Rosenthal and Jacobson (1968), pp. 16-17.

FRANK, J. D. (1963), *Persuasion and Healing*, Schocken Books, New York.

FRANK, J. D. (1968), 'The Role of Hope in Psychotherapy', *International Journal of Psychiatry*, vol. 5, pp. 382-412.

FRANK, J. D. (1973), *Persuasion and Healing*, 2nd edn, Johns Hopkins University Press, London and Baltimore.

FRANK, J. D., GLIEDMAN, L. H., IMBER, S. D., NASH, E. H. and STONE, A. R. (1959), 'Patients Expectancies and Relearning as Factors Determining Improvement in Psychotherapy', *American Journal of Psychiatry*, vol. 115, pp. 961-8. See Goldstein (1962) pp. 21-2.

FREUD, S. (1963), *The Complete Psychological Works of Sigmund Freud*, vol. 7, Hogarth Press, London.

FREUD, S. (1963), *Therapy and Technique*, Collier-Macmillan, New York.

GARFIELD SOL, L. (1971), 'Research on Client Variables in Psychotherapy', chapter 8 in Bergin and Garfield (1971).

GLIEDMAN, L. H., NASH, E. H., IMBER, S. D., STONE, A. E. and FRANK, J. D. (1958), 'Reduction of Symptoms by Pharmacologically Inert Substances and by Short Term Psychotherapy', *A.M.A. Archives of Neurological Psychiatry*, vol. 79, pp. 345-51. See Goldstein (1962), pp. 22-3.

GOFFMAN, E. (1968), *Asylums*, Penguin Books, Harmondsworth.

GOFFMAN, E. (1968), *Stigma*, Penguin Books, Harmondsworth.

GOLDSTEIN, A. P. (1960), 'Therapist and Client Expectation of Personality Change in Psychotherapy', *Journal of Counseling Psychology*, vol. 7, pp. 180-4.

GOLDSTEIN, A. P. (1962), *Therapist-Patient Expectancies in Psychotherapy*, Pergamon Press, London.

GOLDSTEIN, A. P. (1973), *Structured Learning Therapy: Toward a Psychotherapy for the Poor*, Academic Press, New York and London.

GOLDSTEIN, A. P. (1975), 'Relationship-Enhancement Methods', chapter 2 of *Helping People Change*, ed. F. M. Kanfer and A. P. Goldstein, Pergamon Press, New York and Oxford.

GOLDSTEIN, A. P. and SHIPMAN, K. (1961), 'Patient's Expectancies, Symptom Reduction, and Aspects of the Initial Psychotherapeutic Interview', *Journal of Clinical Psychology*, vol. 17, pp. 129-33.

Bibliography

GRYGIER, T., CHESLEY, J. and TUTERS, E. W. (1969), 'Parental Deprivation: A Study of Delinquent Children', *British Journal of Criminology,* vol. 9, no. 3.

HALEY, J. (1969), 'The Art of Being a Failure as a Therapist', *American Journal of Orthopsychiatry,* vol. 39, no. 4, pp. 691-5.

HALMOS, P. (1965), *The Faith of the Counsellors,* Constable, London.

HARDIKER, P. (1972), 'Problem Definition: An Interactionist Approach', chapter 4 of *Behaviour Modification in Social Work,* ed. D. Jehu, P. Hardiker, M. Velloly and M. Shaw, John Wiley, London.

HEINE, R. W. (1953), 'A Comparison of Patient's Reports on Psychotherapeutic Experience with Psychoanalytic, Nondirective and Adlerian Therapists', *American Journal of Psychotherapy,* vol. 7, pp. 16-23.

HELLER, K. and GOLDSTEIN, A. P. (1961), 'Client Dependency and Therapist Expectancy as Relationship Maintaining Variables in Psychotherapy', *Journal of Consulting Psychology,* vol. 25, pp. 371-5. See Goldstein (1962), pp. 47-8.

HILGARD, E. R. (1973), 'The Domain of Hypnosis', *American Psychologist,* vol. 28, no. 11, pp. 972-82.

HODGKIN, N. (1973), *New Careers for the Disadvantaged,* NACRO Papers, London.

JUNG, C. G. (1974), Letter 338J in *The Freud-Jung Letters,* Hogarth Press and Routledge & Kegan Paul, London.

JUNG, C. G. (1961), *Freud and Psycho-Analysis,* The Collected Works, vol. 4, Routledge & Kegan Paul, London.

JUNG, C. G. (1933), *Modern Man in Search of a Soul,* Routledge & Kegan Paul, London.

KELLY, G. A. (1955), *The Psychology of Personal Constructs,* vol. 1, Norton, New York.

KIEV, A. (1966), 'Prescientific Psychiatry', chapter 12 of *American Handbook of Psychiatry,* vol. II, ed. S. Arieti, Basic Books, New York.

KOGAN, K. L. and WIMBERGER, H. C. (1971), 'Behaviour Transactions Between Disturbed Children and their Mothers', *Psychology Reports,* vol. 28, pp. 395-404.

KRASNER, L. (1962), 'The Reinforcement Machine', chapter 10 in Berenson and Carkhuff (1967).

KRASNER, L. and ULLMAN, L. P. (1973), *Behavior Influence and Personality,* Holt, Rinehart & Winston, New York and London.

LAING, R. D. (1969a), *The Self and Others,* 2nd edn, Tavistock, London.

LAING, R. D. (1969b), *Intervention in Social Situations,* The Association of Family Caseworkers, London. (Reprinted 1971 by the Philadelphia Association Ltd.)

LERNER, B. and FISKE, D. W. (1973), 'Clients' Attributes and the Eye of the Beholder', *Journal of Consulting and Clinical Psychology,* vol. 40, pp. 272-7.

LIPKIN, S. (1954), 'Client's Feelings and Attitudes in Relation to the Outcome of Client-Centered Therapy', *Psychological Monographs,* vol. 68.

McREYNOLDS, W. T., BARNES, A. R., BROOKS, S. and REMAGEN, N. J. (1973), 'The Role of Attention—Placebo Influences in the Efficacy of Systematic Desensitization', *Journal of Consulting and Clinical Psychology,* vol. 41, pp. 86-92.

Bibliography

MALAN, D. H. (1973), 'The Outcome Problem in Psychotherapy Research', *Archives of General Psychiatry,* vol. 29, pp. 719-29.

MARCIA, J. E., RUBIN, B. M. and EFRAN, J. S. (1969), 'Systematic Desensitization: Expectancy Change or Countercondition?' *Journal of Abnormal Psychology,* vol. 74, pp. 382-7.

MAY, P. R. A. (1971), 'For Better or for Worse? Psychotherapy and Variance Change: A Critical Preview of the Literature', *Journal of Nervous and Mental Disease,* vol. 152, pp. 184-92.

MEICHENBAUM, D. M., BOWERS, K. S. and ROSS, R. R. (1969), 'A Behavioural Analysis of Teacher Expectancy Effect', *Journal of Personal and Social Psychology,* vol. 13, no. 4, pp. 306-16.

MEICHENBAUM, D. M. and SMART, I. (1971), 'Use of Direct Expectancy to Modify Academic Performance and Attitudes of College Students', *Journal of Counseling Psychology,* vol. 18, no. 6, pp. 531-5.

MENNINGER, K. (1964), Review of J. S. Bockoven, *Moral Treatment in American Psychiatry* (Springer, New York, 1963), *Bulletin of the Menninger Clinic,* vol. 28, pp. 274-5. Quoted in Rosenthal and Jacobson (1968), p. 13.

MERTON, R. K. (1948), 'The Self Fulfilling Prophecy', *Antioch Review,* vol. 8, pp. 193-210.

MERTON, R. K. (1968), *Social Theory and Social Structure,* Free Press, New York, pp. 475-88.

MURRAY, E. J. (1956), 'A Content-Analysis Method for Studying Psychotherapy', *Psychological Monographs,* vol. 70, p. 13. See Murray and Jacobson (1971), p. 720.

MURRAY, E. J. and JACOBSON, L. I. (1971), 'The Nature of Learning in Traditional and Behavioral Psychotherapy', chapter 18 in Bergin and Garfield (1971).

ORNE, M. T. (1962), 'On the Social Psychology of the Psychological Experiments: With Particular Reference to Demand Characteristics and their Implication', *American Psychologist,* vol. 17, pp. 776-83.

ORNE, M. T. and SCHEIBE, K. E. (1964), 'The Contribution of Non-deprivation Factors in the Production of Sensory Deprivation Effects', *Journal of Abnormal and Social Psychology,* vol. 68, pp. 3-12.

PARK, L. C. and COVI, L. (1965), 'Non-Blind Placebo Trial: An Exploration of Neurotic Patients' Responses to Placebo when its Inert Content is Disclosed', *Archives of General Psychiatry,* vol. 12, pp. 336-45.

PFUNGST, O. (1911), *Clever Hans: A Contribution to Experimental, Animal, and Human Psychology,* trans. C. L. Rahn, Holt, Rinehart & Winston, New York. See Rosenthal (1969), pp. 197-8.

PLATONOV, K. I. (1959), *The Word Factor,* Foreign Languages Publishing House, Moscow.

RACHMAN, S. (1971), *The Effects of Psychotherapy,* Pergamon Press, Oxford.

ROETHLISBERGER, F. J. and DICKSON, W. J. (1939), *Management and the Worker,* Harvard University Press.

ROGERS, C. R. (1946), 'Significant Aspects of Client-Centered Therapy', *American Psychologist,* vol. 1, pp. 415-22. Quoted in Rogers (1966), p. 193.

101

Bibliography

ROGERS, C. R. (1954), 'Changes in the Maturity of Behaviour as Related to Therapy', chapter 13 of *Psychotherapy and Personality Change*, ed. C. R. Rogers and R. F. Dymond, University of Chicago Press.

ROGERS, C. R. (1957), 'The Necessary and Sufficient Conditions of Therapeutic Personality Change', *Journal of Consulting Psychology*, vol. 21, pp. 95-103.

ROGERS, C. R. (1961), *On Becoming a Person*, Houghton Mifflin, Boston.

ROGERS, C. R. (1966), 'Client-Centered Therapy', chapter 13 of *American Handbook of Psychiatry*, vol. 3, ed. S. Arieti, Basic Books, New York.

ROGERS, C. R. and DYMOND, R. F. (1954), *Psychotherapy and Personality Change*, University of Chicago Press.

ROGERS, C. R. (1967) with GENOLIN, E. T., KIESLER, D. and TRUAX, C. B. *The Therapeutic Relationship and its Impact*, University of Wisconsin Press, Madison.

ROSENHAN, D. L. (1973), 'On Being Sane in Insane Places', *Science*, vol. 179, pp. 250-8.

ROSENTHAL, D. (1955), 'Changes in Some Moral Values Following Psychotherapy', *Journal of Consulting Psychology*, vol. 19, no. 6, pp. 431-86.

ROSENTHAL, D. and FRANK, J. D. (1956), 'Psychotherapy and the Placebo Effect', *Psychological Bulletin*, vol. 53, no. 4, pp. 294-302.

ROSENTHAL, R. (1964), 'The Effect of the Experimenter on the Results of Psychological Research', in *Progress in Experimental Personality Research*, vol. 1, ed. B. A. Maher, Academic Press, New York, pp. 79-114.

ROSENTHAL, R. (1966), *Experimenter Effects in Behavioural Research*, Appleton-Century-Crofts, New York.

ROSENTHAL, R. (1969), 'Interpersonal Expectations: Effects of the Experimenter's Hypothesis', chapter 6 of *Artifact in Behavioural Research*, ed. R. Rosenthal and R. L. Rosnow, Academic Press, New York.

ROSENTHAL, R. and JACOBSON, E. (1968), *Pygmalion in the Classroom*, Holt, Rinehart & Winston, New York.

RUBINGTON, E. and WEINBERG, H. S. (1973), *Deviance: The Interactionist Perspective*, 2nd edn, Macmillan, New York, Collier-Macmillan, London.

RUBOVITS, P. C. and MAEHR, M. L. (1971), 'Pygmalion Analyzed', *Journal of Personal and Social Psychology*, vol. 19, no. 2, pp. 197-203.

RYCHLAK (1968), *A Philosophy of Science for Personality Theory*, Houghton Mifflin, Boston.

SARGENT, W. (1957), *Battle for the Mind: A Physiology of Conversion and Brain-Washing*, Heinemann, London.

SCHEFF, T. J. (1968), 'Negotiating Reality: Notes on Power in the Assessment of Responsibility', *Social Problems* No. 16, pp. 3-18.

SCHEFF, T. J. (1975), *Labeling Madness*, Prentice-Hall, Englewood Cliffs, N.J.

SCHMALE A. H. (1969), 'The Importance of Life Setting for Disease Onset', *Modern Treatment*, vol. 6, no. 4, July.

SCHMALE, A. H. and IKER, H. (1965), 'The Psychological Setting of Uterine Cervical Cancer', paper presented to New York Academy of Sciences, 5 April 1965.

SELIGMAN, M. E. P. (1975), *Helplessness*, Freeman, San Francisco.

SHAPIRO, A. K. (1960), 'A Contribution to a History of the Placebo Effect', *Behavioural Science*, vol. V, pp. 109-35.

SHAPIRO, A. K. (1971), 'Placebo Effects in Medicine, Psychotherapy and Psychoanalysis', chapter 12 in Bergin and Garfield (1971).

SHEASBY, E. A. (1971), 'A Study of the Diagnosis and Treatment of Clients Recommended Positively for and Negatively against Probation as Recorded in Official Files', unpub. dissertation, Sussex University.

SNOW, R. E. (1969), 'Unfinished Pygmalion', *Contemporary Psychology*, vol. 14, no. 4, pp. 197-9.

SPANOS, N. P. and BARBER, T. X. (1974), 'Toward a Convergence in Hypnosis Research', *American Psychologist*, vol. 29, no. 7, pp. 500-11.

STRUPP, H. H. (1958), 'The Performance of Psychiatrists and Psychologists in a Therapeutic Interview', *Journal of Clinical Psychology*, vol. 14, pp. 219-26.

STRUPP, H. H. (1960), 'Nature of Psychotherapists' Contributions to the Treatment Process', *Archives of General Psychiatry*, vol. 3, pp. 219-31.

STRUPP, H. H. (1962), *Research in Psychotherapy*, vol. 2, ed. H. H. Strupp and L. Luborsky, American Psychological Association, Washington.

STRUPP, H. H. (1970), 'Specific-v-Nonspecific Factors in Psychotherapy', *Archives of General Psychiatry*, vol. 23, pp. 393-401.

STRUPP, H. H. (1973), 'On the Basic Ingredients of Psychotherapy', *Journal of Consulting and Clinical Psychology*, vol. 41, no. 1, pp. 1-8.

STRUPP, H. H. and WILLIAMS, J. V. (1960), 'Some Determinants of Clinical Evaluations of Different Psychiatrists', *Archives of General Psychiatry*, vol. 2, pp. 432-40. See Goldstein (1972), p. 51.

TEMERLIN, M. K. (1968), 'Suggestion Effects in Psychiatric Diagnosis', *Journal of Nervous and Mental Disease*, vol. 147, pp. 349-58.

TRUAX, C. B. (1960), 'Reinforcement and non-Reinforcement in Rogerian Psychotherapy', *Journal of Abnormal and Social Psychology*, vol. 71, no. 1, pp. 1-9. See Truax and Carkhuff (1967), pp. 158-9.

TRUAX, C. B. (1963), 'Effective Ingredients in Psychotherapy: An Approach to Unraveling the Patient-Therapist Interaction', *Journal of Counseling Psychology*, vol. 10, pp. 256-63.

TRUAX, C. B. and CARKHUFF, R. R. (1964), 'New Directions in Clinical Research', pp. 358-91 in Berenson and Carkhuff (1967).

TRUAX, C. B. and CARKHUFF, R. R. (1967), *Toward Effective Counseling and Psychotherapy*, Aldine, Chicago.

TRUAX, C. B. and MITCHELL, K. M. (1971), 'Research on Certain Therapist Interpersonal Skills in Relation to Process and Outcome', chapter 9 in Bergin and Garfield (1971).

WALLACH, M. S. and STRUPP, H. H. (1960), 'Psychotherapists' Clinical Judgements and Attitudes Toward Patients', *Journal of Consulting Psychology*, vol. 24, pp. 316-23. See Goldstein (1972), pp. 51-52.

WOLFF, W. (1954), 'Fact and Value in Psychotherapy', *American Journal of Psychotherapy*, vol. 8, pp. 466-86.

WRENN, R. L. (1960), 'Counselor Orientation: Theoretical or Situational?', *Journal of Counseling Psychology*, vol. 7, pp. 40-45. See Truax and Carkhuff (1964), p. 370.